THE
AMERICAN REVOLUTION
AND THE
YOUNG REPUBLIC
1763 to 1816

DOCUMENTING AMERICA
THE PRIMARY SOURCE DOCUMENTS OF A NATION

THE AMERICAN REVOLUTION AND THE YOUNG REPUBLIC

1763 to 1816

EDITED BY JEFF WALLENFELDT, MANAGER, GEOGRAPHY AND HISTORY

Britannica®
Educational Publishing

IN ASSOCIATION WITH

ROSEN
EDUCATIONAL SERVICES

Published in 2012 by Britannica Educational Publishing
(a trademark of Encyclopædia Britannica, Inc.)
in association with Rosen Educational Services, LLC
29 East 21st Street, New York, NY 10010.

Distributed exclusively by Rosen Educational Services.
For a listing of additional Britannica Educational Publishing titles, call toll free (800) 237-9932.

First Edition

Britannica Educational Publishing
Michael I. Levy: Executive Editor
Marilyn L. Barton: Senior Coordinator, Production Control
Steven Bosco: Director, Editorial Technologies
Lisa S. Braucher: Senior Producer and Data Editor
Yvette Charboneau: Senior Copy Editor
Kathy Nakamura: Manager, Media Acquisition
Jeff Wallenfeldt: Manager, Geography and History

Rosen Educational Services
Heather M. Moore Niver: Editor
Nelson Sá: Art Director
Cindy Reiman: Photography Manager
Karen Huang: Photo Researcher
Matthew Cauli: Cover Design
Brian Garvey: Designer
Introduction by Jeff Wallenfeldt

Library of Congress Cataloging-in-Publication Data

The American Revolution and the young Republic, 1763 to 1816 / edited by Jeff Wallenfeldt.
    p. cm.—(Documenting America : the primary source documents of a nation)
Includes bibliographical references and index.
ISBN 978-1-61530-668-8 (library binding)
1. United States—History—Colonial period, 1600-1775—Sources. 2. United States—History—Revolution, 1775-1783—Sources. 3. United States—History—1783-1815—Sources. I. Wallenfeldt, Jeffrey H.
E173.A7537 2012
973.2—dc23

                                                                    2011021358

Manufactured in the United States of America

On the cover: Rendering by William Barnes Wollen of the Battle of Lexington, which took place on April 19th, 1775. *The Bridgeman Art Library/Getty Images*. **(Background and back cover)** The Declaration of of Independence. *National Archives, Washington, D.C.*

On pages viii-ix: The U.S. Constitution was signed on Sept. 17, 1787; painting by Howard Chandler Christy. © *SuperStock*

On pages 1, 14, 24, 31, 41, 51, 58: The Liberty Bell, now a national symbol of freedom, was commissioned in 1751 and can still be viewed at Independence National Historic Park in Philadelphia, PA. *Shutterstock.com*

CONTENTS

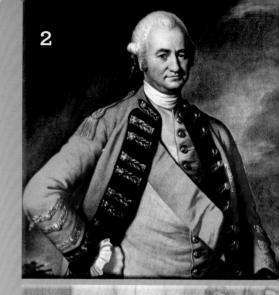

46

57

62

69

One's understanding of any period of history is always deepened by close examination of primary sources. The careful description and reasoned discussion of most historiography allows the student of history to make sense of issues and ideals, but primary source accounts bring them vividly to life. Concepts and events that are often conveyed with academic equanimity in a historical narrative can seem to be shouted in primary sources, in which the frustration, determination, and dreams of historical actors surge off the page. Yet this up-close, often visceral experience of history can remain largely incomprehensible if it is not grounded in context. Linear history establishes when events occurred relative to one another, and the thematic interpretation of history offers an explanation of why events occurred. Bringing all these approaches together, this volume offers the opportunity for a multidimensional experience of history. Punctuated with excerpts from some of the era's most revealing primary sources (which can be read more fully in the Appendices), this account of American history—from the run-up to the Revolution to the early years of the Republic—allows the reader to see the period in panoramic widescreen as well as with fly-on-the-wall intimacy. Each primary source document also includes an introduction that provides additional context.

"No taxation without representation," "We hold these truths to be self-evident," "We the People of the United States": few phrases echo as loudly or resonate as meaningfully in the halls of American history as do these from the time of the country's founding. As much as the personal statements provided in this volume, the political documents offered here—the declarations, resolutions, and legislation—speak loudly for this crucial period. They are the voice of the many, the Founders and the faithful, chiming together to proclaim the needs of a people who defied a great Empire. They are the transcript of the protests, the planning, and the negotiations that launched the American experiment in republican democracy.

The end of the Great War for the Empire (the French and Indian War), fought from 1754 to 1763, was in many ways the beginning of the American Revolution. As a result of Britain's triumph in the war, its North American colonies had swelled to include not just Canada but large tracts of land reaching westward to the Mississippi River. This acquisition, however, had come at great cost to the British government. Fighting a war on the high seas and several continents was not cheap. Parliament decided that the colonies should share the cost and initiated a series of taxes.

The first of these taxes, generally referred to as the Sugar Act, which came in 1764, brought much grumbling but general acquiescence from the colonists, as did the Currency Act. The Stamp Act of 1765, an "internal" tax on legal documents, newspapers advertisements, and a variety of other transactions, was a different matter, sparking a defiant uproar from colonists. Although "sincerely devoted with the warmest sentiments of affection and duty to His Majesty's person and government," the members of the Stamp Act Congress made clear that they felt their rights as Englishmen had been violated by "taxation without representation." Member of Parliament Soame Jenyns countered that the colonists, like all nonlandholders in England who could not vote, had "virtual representation" in Parliament. Ultimately, fearing the consequences of a colonial embargo on British goods, Parliament rescinded the tax but immediately enacted the muscle-flexing Declaratory Act, which more or less announced that Parliament had the right to legislate for the colonies in whatever manner it chose. The Townshend duties of 1767, "external" taxes on a variety of goods, made this point and again outraged the colonists. Although the duties were repealed in 1770, tensions continued to escalate with the increased presence of British troops, leading to the Boston Massacre and the best-known "party" in American history in response to the Tea Act of 1773: the Boston Tea Party.

In October 1774, determined to put an end to a series of new British-imposed measures they called the "Intolerable Acts," colonial representatives met as the First Continental Congress. This time "His Majesty's most loyal subjects … affected with the deepest anxiety and most alarming apprehensions at those grievances and distresses, with which His Majesties American subjects are oppressed," threatened to cut off trade with Britain. In the wake of fighting between British troops and colonial Minutemen at Lexington and Concord, Mass., in April 1775, the Congress, still hopeful of reconciliation, set forth in July the "Causes and Necessity of Their Taking up Arms," stating that "our attachment to no nation upon earth should supplant our attachment to liberty," and that "we are reduced to the alternative of choosing an unconditional submission to the tyranny of irritated ministers or resistance by force." In *Common Sense*, a widely read political pamphlet published in January 1776, Thomas Paine questioned the logic of filial loyalty to Britain: "Europe, and not England, is the parent country of America," he wrote. "This New World has been the asylum for the persecuted lovers of civil and religious liberty from *every* part of Europe," he added, on his way to concluding that "Everything that is right or natural pleads for separation. The blood of the slain, the weeping voice of nature cries, 'tis time to part.'"

By the summer of 1776 the delegates to the Continental Congress agreed, tasking a committee comprising Benjamin Franklin, John Adams, Thomas Jefferson, Roger Sherman, and Robert R. Livingston with drafting a formal statement of separation. The Declaration of Independence was primarily the work of Jefferson, who not only enumerated "a long train of abuses and usurpations" but provided a road map for democracy, though the Declaration's now familiar language seems to have come from a well-spring of American identity somewhere beneath Independence Hall in Philadelphia, where it was approved by the Congress on July 4.

Having declared independence, the Americans were faced with the challenge of winning it in battle against the 18th-century world's dominant military power. While there were some successes for the Americans early in the war, Gen. George Washington's leadership of the American forces was uncertain initially, and the British distinctly had the upper hand. Still, stealth and surprise worked to Washington's advantage at Trenton and Princeton, N.J., in late 1776 and reinvigorated the American war effort. The following winter, while the beleaguered Continental Army licked its wounds at Valley Forge, Penn., Washington's aide Alexander Hamilton wrote Congress, under Washington's name, and outlined military reforms he felt were necessary if the Americans were to fight on effectively. In time the Americans were aided by the Dutch, the Spanish, and especially the French, the last of whom played a major role in the siege of the British forces at Yorktown, Va. The siege sealed ultimate victory for the United States through the Treaty of Paris in 1783.

From 1781 to 1789, the country operated under the Articles of Confederation, which bound the states together but provided neither for control over taxes and trade nor a federal executive and judiciary, though they prohibited "the United States in Congress assembled, or any of them," from granting "any title of nobility." The stability of this loosely federative arrangement was tested by periodic upheavals such as Shays's Rebellion in Massachusetts in 1786–87, in which disenchanted debtors rioted. With the ratification of the Constitution in 1789, the states were solidly linked by one of the world's landmark documents in a federal union. A series of compromises had to be negotiated, however, before agreement was reached on this, the fundamental law of the U.S. system of government. Not the least of these compromises was the implied acceptance of slavery—an institution many founders abhorred—through the codification of slaves as three-fifths of a person for purposes of determining representation in Congress and through prohibiting Congress from banning the importation of slaves until 1808. As the Southern states were appeased in the interest of unity, deaf ears were turned to appeals, such as the petitions for equality under the law by Africans Americans in Charleston, S.C., in 1791.

But while it would be nearly 100 years before the Constitution would be amended to guarantee African Americans their freedom and civil rights, its first 10 amendments, known as the Bill of Rights, set forth in 1789 a litany of protections against government encroachment that had been assumed but were now guaranteed. However, disagreements over interpretation of them and the Constitution as a whole would remain at the centre of American dialogue. As early as 1775, Abigail Adams wrote a letter to her husband, the future second president John Adams, in which she despaired speculatively at the nature of the American government to come: "I am more and more convinced that man is a dangerous creature; and that power, whether vested in many or a few, is ever grasping....The great fish swallow up the small; and he who is most strenuous for the rights of the people when vested with power, is as eager after the prerogatives of government." The Constitution of Vermont, enacted in 1777, reflected those adopted by other states, the bulk of it copied from the constitution of Pennsylvania. Its preamble, declaring Vermont's separation from New York state, echoed the Declaration of Independence in proclaiming that "whenever those great ends of government are not obtained, the people have a right, by common consent, to change it" and in protesting the difficulty of legislating at a distance: "upward of 450 miles from the seat of that government, which renders it extreme difficult to continue under the jurisdiction of said state."

Here is the centrifugal tendency that had pulled the states in the direction of sovereignty that would thereafter be trumpeted as states' rights. The opposite centripetal force, federalism, drew them together and empowered the central government. Its case was eloquently articulated in a series of essays published in newspapers in 1787–88 by Alexander Hamilton, James Madison, and John Jay. Collectively, these impassioned arguments for the benefits of good, republican government came to be known as the *Federalist Papers*. "An overscrupulous jealousy of danger to the rights of the people, which is more commonly the fault of the head than of the heart," wrote Hamilton in *The Federalist* No. 1, "will be represented as mere pretense and artifice, the stale bait for popularity at the expense of public good." The tension between these two viewpoints gave rise to the country's first political parties, the Federalists and the Democratic-Republicans, led by Jefferson, a political division that Washington, the country's first president, bemoaned in his 1796 Farewell Address.

In 1803 the territory of the United States ballooned with the Louisiana Purchase, a huge expanse of land from the Mississippi to the Rocky Mountains and from the Gulf of Mexico to Canada, bought from France under the aegis of Jefferson as the third president. Uncertain of the constitutional authority of his executive action, Jefferson defended it in letters to his confidant John Breckinridge, even as he prepared an amendment to the Constitution to codify it. The free practice of religion, which remained central to American nationhood, was again reinvigorated by renewed devotion during the Second Great Awakening in this period. Protestant denominations multiplied, but at the same time there was a movement among some denominations to combine their efforts, as can be seen in the Plan for Union of 1801. American Christians also continued to reach out spiritually to the Indians, though the Native Americans often did not welcome this proselytizing, a response that was succinctly summarized by the Seneca Chief Red Jacket in 1805: "Brother, we do not wish to destroy your religion or take it from you. We only want to enjoy our own."

And so the young American republic endeavoured to make its way in the world. Its people were far from agreement on many issues, but they had chosen to pledge to each other their lives, their fortunes, and their sacred honour. Their nationhood and their mutual resolve would be tested again in another conflict with Britain, the War of 1812, called by some the Second American Revolution. The war was effectively a draw, but it secured the place of the United States of America in the world order.

CHAPTER 1

PRELUDE TO REVOLUTION

Although Britain and France had technically been at peace since 1748, both powers continued to harass each other in their colonial settlements in North America, the West Indies, and India. When the French attacked the British colony of Minorca in May 1756, war broke out; Britain allied itself with Prussia and France with Austria. The war (the North American component of which is known as both the Great War for the Empire and the French and Indian War) began badly for Britain; it lost Oswego in North America as well as Minorca. By 1757, however, under the leadership of Thomas Pelham-Holmes, 1st duke of Newcastle, and William Pitt, the Elder, the tide began to turn. Victory came first in India, where Britain and France were keen competitors. Gen. Robert Clive captured the French settlement of Chandernagore and then, with the forces of the East India Company, defeated the army of Siraj al-Dawlah, the ruler of Bengal, at the Battle of Plassey on June 23, 1757. That year is often cited as the beginning of Britain's supremacy over India, the start of Calcutta's significance as the headquarters of the East India Company, and the beginning of the end of French influence on the

Gen. Robert Clive won the Battle of Plassey for the British on June 23, 1757. Hulton Archive/Getty Images

subcontinent. Two years later large sections of the French fleet were destroyed at the naval battle of Quiberon Bay, off the coast of France. When Quebec fell to Gen. James Wolfe in 1759, British control of Canada was effectively secured.

In the short term these victories resulted in a mood of patriotic exultation, especially among British merchants. They looked to the new colonies to provide both fresh stocks of raw materials and eager markets for British manufactured goods: "Trade," British statesman Edmund Burke gloated, "had been made to flourish by war." The conquest of Canada freed the American colonists

from the fear of a French invasion from the north. Anxiety on this score had helped to foster American attachment to Britain. Now these fears had been relieved, and as early as 1760 some Britons and Americans anticipated that this would lead to difficulties.

NORTH AMERICA AFTER THE GREAT WAR FOR THE EMPIRE

Britain's victory over France in the Great War for the Empire had been won at very great cost. British government expenditures, which had amounted to nearly £6.5 million annually before the war, rose to about £14.5 million annually during the war. As a result, the burden of taxation in England was probably the highest in the country's history, much of it borne by the politically influential landed classes. Furthermore, with the acquisition of the vast domain of Canada and the prospect of holding British territories both against the various nations of Indians and against the Spaniards to the south and west, the costs of colonial defense could be expected to continue indefinitely. Parliament, moreover, had voted to give Massachusetts a generous sum in compensation for its war expenses. It therefore seemed reasonable to British opinion that some of the future burden of payment should be shifted to the colonists themselves—who until then had been lightly taxed and indeed lightly governed.

The prolonged wars had also revealed the need to tighten the administration of the loosely run and widely scattered elements of the British Empire. If the course of the war had confirmed the necessity, the end of the war presented the opportunity. The acquisition of Canada required officials in London to take responsibility for the unsettled western territories, now freed from the threat of French occupation. The British soon moved to take charge of the whole field of Indian relations. By the royal Proclamation of 1763, a line was drawn down the Appalachians marking the limit of settlement from the British colonies, beyond which Indian trade was to be conducted strictly through British-appointed commissioners. The proclamation sprang in part from a respect for Indian rights (though it did not come in time to prevent the uprising led by Pontiac). From London's viewpoint, leaving a lightly garrisoned West to the fur-gathering Indians also made economic and imperial sense. The proclamation, however, caused consternation among British colonists for two reasons. It meant that limits were being set to the prospects of settlement and speculation in western lands, and it took control of the west out of colonial hands. The most ambitious men in the colonies thus saw the proclamation as a loss of power to control their own fortunes. Indeed, the British government's huge underestimation of how deeply the halt in westward expansion would be resented by the colonists was one of the factors in sparking the 12-year crisis that led to the American Revolution. Indian efforts to preserve a terrain for themselves in the continental interior might still have had a chance with British policy makers, but they would be totally ineffective when the time came to deal with a triumphant United States of America.

THE TAX CONTROVERSY

George Grenville, who was named prime minister in 1763, was soon looking to meet the costs of defense by

George Grenville's taxation of the colonies was so severe that it instigated events that led to the American Revolution. Act Hulton Archive/Getty Images

raising revenue in the colonies. The first measure was the Plantation Act of 1764, usually called the Revenue, or Sugar, Act, which reduced to a mere three-pence the duty on imported foreign molasses but linked with this a high duty on refined sugar and a prohibition on foreign rum (the needs of the British treasury were carefully balanced with those of West Indies planters and New England distillers). The last measure of this kind (1733) had not been enforced, but this time the government set up a system of customs houses, staffed by British officers, and even established a vice-admiralty court. The court sat at Halifax, N.S., and heard very few cases, but in principle it appeared to threaten the cherished British privilege of trials by local juries. Boston further objected to the tax's revenue-raising aspect on constitutional grounds, but, despite some expressions of anxiety, the colonies in general acquiesced.

Parliament next affected colonial economic prospects by passing a Currency Act (1764) to withdraw paper currencies, many of them surviving from the war period, from circulation. This was not done to restrict economic growth so much as to take out currency that was thought to be unsound, but it did severely reduce the circulating medium during the difficult postwar period and further indicated that such matters were subject to British control.

Grenville's next move was a stamp duty, to be raised on a wide variety of transactions, including legal writs,

newspaper advertisements, and ships' bills of lading. The colonies were duly consulted and offered no alternative suggestions. The feeling in London, shared by Benjamin Franklin, was that, after making formal objections, the colonies would accept the new taxes as they had the earlier ones. But the Stamp Act (1765) hit harder and deeper than any previous parliamentary measure. As some agents had already pointed out, because of postwar economic difficulties the colonies were short of ready funds. (In Virginia this shortage was so serious that the province's treasurer, John Robinson, who was also speaker of the assembly, manipulated and redistributed paper money that had been officially withdrawn from circulation by the Currency Act; a large proportion of the landed gentry benefited from this largesse.) The Stamp Act struck at vital points of colonial economic operations, affecting transactions in trade. It also affected many of the most articulate and influential people in the colonies (lawyers, journalists, bankers). It was, moreover, the first "internal" tax levied directly on the colonies by Parliament. Previous colonial taxes had been levied by local authorities or had been "external" import duties whose primary aim could be viewed as regulating trade for the benefit of the empire as a whole rather than raising revenue. Yet no one, either in Britain or in the colonies, fully anticipated the uproar that followed the imposition of these duties. Mobs in Boston and other towns rioted and

Document: No Taxation Without Representation (1765)

Formal opposition to the Stamp Act led to the October 1765 Stamp Act Congress in New York. Delegates from nine colonies convened and wrote a moderate statement of colonial rights. In addition to the adoption of "The Declarations" on October 19, the delegates prepared petitions to the king, the House of Lords, and the House of Commons. Because the members of the congress were far more conservative in their sentiments than colonial legislatures had been, some delegates refused to sign even the moderate documents that were produced by the congress. Parliament rejected the petitions in spite of their mildness. The Stamp Act Congress was the first intercolonial congress to meet in America. It was a foundation from which the subsequent Continental congresses arose.

The Congress met according to adjournment, and resumed, etc., as yesterday. And upon mature deliberation agreed to the following declarations of the rights and grievances of the colonists, in America, which were ordered to be inserted.

The members of this Congress, sincerely devoted with the warmest sentiments of affection and duty to His Majesty's person and government, inviolably attached to the present happy establishment of the Protestant succession, and with minds deeply impressed by a sense of the present and impending misfortunes of the British colonies on this continent, having considered as maturely as time will permit the circumstances of the said colonies, esteem it our indispensable duty to make the following declarations of our humble opinion, respecting the most essential rights and liberties of the colonists, and of the grievances under which they labor, by reason of several late acts of Parliament.

- That His Majesty's subjects in these colonies owe the same allegiance to the Crown of Great Britain that is owing from his subjects born within the Realm, and all due subordination to that august body, the Parliament of Great Britain.
- That His Majesty's liege subjects in these colonies are entitled to all the inherent rights and liberties of his natural-born subjects within the Kingdom of Great Britain.
- That it is inseparably essential to the freedom of a people, and the undoubted right of Englishmen, that no taxes be imposed on them but with their own consent, given personally or by their representatives.
- That the people of these colonies are not, and, from their local circumstances, cannot be represented in the House of Commons in Great Britain....

forced appointed stamp distributors to renounce their posts; legal business was largely halted. Several colonies sent delegations to a Congress in New York in the summer of 1765, where the Stamp Act was denounced as a violation of the Englishman's right to be taxed only through elected representatives, and plans were adopted to impose a nonimportation embargo on British goods.

A mocking skull and crossbones version of the official stamp required by the Stamp Act of 1756. Library of Congress Prints and Photographs Division

A change of ministry facilitated a change of British policy on taxation. Parliamentary opinion was angered by what it perceived as colonial lawlessness, but British merchants were worried about the embargo on British imports. The marquis of Rockingham, succeeding Grenville, was persuaded to repeal the Stamp Act—for domestic reasons rather than out of any sympathy with colonial protests—and in 1766 the repeal was passed. On the same day, however, Parliament also passed the Declaratory Act, which declared that Parliament had

the power to bind or legislate the colonies "in all cases whatsoever." Parliament would not have voted the repeal without this assertion of its authority.

The colonists, jubilant at the repeal of the Stamp Act, drank innumerable toasts, sounded peals of cannon, and were prepared to ignore the Declaratory Act as face-saving window dressing. John Adams, however, warned in his *Dissertation on the Canon and Feudal Law* that Parliament, armed with this view of its powers, would try to tax the colonies again. This happened in 1767 when Charles Townshend became chancellor of the Exchequer in a ministry formed by Pitt, now earl of Chatham. The problem was that Britain's financial burden had not been lifted. Townshend, claiming to take literally the colonial distinction between external and internal taxes, imposed external duties on a wide range of necessities, including lead, glass, paint, paper, and tea, the principal domestic beverage. One ominous result was that colonists now began to believe that the British were developing a long-term plan to reduce the colonies to a subservient position, which they were soon calling "slavery." This view was ill-informed, however. Grenville's measures had been designed as a carefully considered package. Apart from some tidying-up legislation, Grenville had had no further plans for the colonies after the Stamp Act. His successors developed further measures, not as extensions of an original plan but because the Stamp Act had been repealed.

To the PUBLIC.

AS I am convinced that my refusing to store my Goods, was wrong; I do promise and consent, That they shall be deposited in the public Store with other Goods which were imported contrary to the *Non-importation Agreement*;---which I hope will appease the Minds of my injured Fellow Citizens, and convince them that I do not regard sacrificing my private Interest for the *Good of the Public*.

Simeon Coley.

New-York, 21st July, 1769.
Afternoon, 2 o'Clock.

A notice to the public from silversmith Simeon Coley regarding the duties imposed by Lord Townshend. Library of Congress, Washington, D.C.

John Dickinson, portrait by Charles Willson Peale, 1770; in Independence National Historical Park, Philadelphia. Courtesy of the Independence National Historical Park Collection, Philadelphia

Nevertheless, the colonists were outraged. In Pennsylvania the lawyer and legislator John Dickinson wrote a series of essays that, appearing in 1767 and 1768 as *Letters from a Farmer in Pennsylvania*, were widely reprinted and exerted great influence in forming a united colonial opposition. Dickinson agreed that Parliament had supreme power where the whole empire was concerned, but he denied that it had power over internal colonial affairs. He quietly implied that the basis of colonial loyalty lay in its utility among equals rather than in obedience owed to a superior.

It proved easier to unite on opinion than on action. Gradually, after much maneuvering and negotiation, a wide-ranging nonimportation policy against British goods was brought into operation. Agreement had not been easy to reach, and the tensions sometimes broke out in acrimonious charges of noncooperation. In addition, the policy had to be enforced by newly created local committees, a process that put a new disciplinary power in the hands of local men who had not had much previous experience in public affairs. There were, as a result, many signs of discontent with the ordering of domestic affairs in some of the colonies—a development that had obvious implications for the future of colonial politics if more action was needed later.

CONSTITUTIONAL DIFFERENCES WITH BRITAIN

Very few colonists wanted or even envisaged independence at this stage. (Dickinson had hinted at such a possibility with expressions of pain that were obviously sincere.) The colonial struggle for power, although charged with intense feeling, was not an attempt to change government structure but an argument over legal interpretation. The core of the colonial case was that, as British subjects, they were entitled to the same privileges as their fellow subjects in Britain. They could not constitutionally be taxed without their own consent; and, because they were unrepresented in the Parliament that voted the taxes, they had not given this consent. James Otis, in two long pamphlets, ceded all sovereign power to Parliament with this proviso. Others, however, began to question whether Parliament did have lawful power to legislate over the colonies. These doubts were expressed by the late 1760s, when James Wilson, a Scottish immigrant lawyer living in Philadelphia, wrote an essay on the subject. Because of the withdrawal of the Townshend round of duties in 1770, Wilson kept this essay private until new troubles arose in 1774, when he published it as *Considerations on the Nature and Extent of the Legislative Authority of the British Parliament*. In this he fully articulated a view that had been gathering force in the colonies (it was also the opinion of Franklin) that Parliament's lawful sovereignty stopped at the shores of Britain.

The official British reply to the colonial case on representation was that the colonies were "virtually" represented in Parliament in the same sense that the large voteless majority of the British public was represented by those who did vote. To this Otis snorted that, if the majority of the British people did not have the vote, they ought to have it. The idea of colonial members of Parliament, several times suggested, was never a likely solution because of problems of time and distance and because, from the colonists' point of view, colonial members would not have adequate influence.

The standpoints of the two sides to the controversy could be traced in the language used. The principle of parliamentary sovereignty was expressed in the language of paternalistic authority; the British referred to themselves as parents and to the colonists as children. Colonial Tories, who accepted Parliament's case in the interests of social stability, also used this terminology. From this point of view, colonial insubordination was "unnatural," just as the revolt of children against parents was unnatural.

James Otis, portrait by J. Blackburn, 1755; in the Library of Congress, Washington, D.C. Courtesy of the Library of Congress, Washington, D.C.

Document: Soame Jenyns: The Objections to the Taxation of Our American Colonies Considered (1765)

Part of the American opposition to British taxation was based on the objection that, because the colonies were not represented in Parliament, that body had no right either to tax them or to legislate for them generally. One member of Parliament, Soame Jenyns, attempted to answer this argument with a theory of "virtual representation." His pamphlet on the objections to colonial taxation, excerpted here, was published in 1765.

The right of the legislature of Great Britain to impose taxes on her American colonies, and the expediency of exerting that right in the present conjuncture, are propositions so indisputably clear that I should never have thought it necessary to have undertaken their defense had not many arguments been lately flung out, both in papers and conversation, which with insolence equal to their absurdity deny them both. As these are usually mixed up with several patriotic and favorite words, such as liberty, property, Englishmen, etc., which are apt to make strong impressions on that more numerous part of mankind who have ears but no understanding, it will not, I think, be improper to give them some answers. To this, therefore, I shall singly confine myself, and do it in as few words as possible. ...

The great capital argument, which I find on this subject, and which, like an elephant at the head of a Nabob's army, being once overthrown must put the whole into confusion, is this: that no Englishman is or can be taxed but by his own consent, by which must be meant one of these three propositions—either that no Englishman can be taxed without his own consent as an individual; or that no Englishman can be taxed without the consent of the persons he chooses to represent him; or that no Englishman can be taxed without the consent of the majority of all those who are elected by himself and others of his fellow subjects to represent them. Now, let us impartially consider whether any of these propositions are in fact true. If not, then this wonderful structure which has been erected upon them falls at once to the ground, and like another Babel perishes by a confusion of words, which the builders themselves are unable to understand....

The colonists replied to all this in the language of rights. They held that Parliament could do nothing in the colonies that it could not do in Britain because the Americans were protected by all the common-law rights of the British. (When the First Continental Congress met in September 1774, one of its first acts was to affirm that the colonies were entitled to the common law of England.)

Rights, as Richard Bland of Virginia insisted in *The Colonel Dismounted* (as early as 1764), implied equality. And here he touched on the underlying source of colonial grievance. Americans were being treated as unequals, which they resented and also feared would lead to a loss of control of their own affairs. Colonists perceived legal inequality when writs of assistance—essentially, general search warrants—were authorized in Boston in 1761 while closely related "general warrants" were outlawed in two celebrated cases in Britain. Townshend specifically legalized writs of assistance in the colonies in 1767. Dickinson devoted one of his *Letters from a Farmer* to this issue.

When Lord North became prime minister early in 1770, George III had at last found a minister who could work both with himself and with Parliament. British government began to acquire some stability. In 1770, in the face of the American policy of nonimportation, the Townshend tariffs were withdrawn—all except the tax on tea, which was kept for symbolic reasons. Relative calm returned, though it was ruffled on the New England coastline by frequent incidents of defiance of customs officers, who could get no support from local juries. These outbreaks did not win much sympathy from other colonies, but they were serious enough to call for an increase in the number of British regular forces stationed in Boston. One of the most violent clashes occurred in Boston just before the repeal of the Townshend duties. Threatened by mob harassment, a small British detachment opened fire and killed five people, an incident soon known as the Boston Massacre. The soldiers were charged with murder and were given a civilian trial, in which John Adams conducted a successful defense.

The other serious quarrel with British authority occurred in New York, where the assembly refused to accept all the

Lord North, detail of a portrait by Sir Nathaniel Dance-Holland; in the National Portrait Gallery, London. Courtesy of the National Portrait Gallery, London

British demands for quartering troops. Before a compromise was reached, Parliament had threatened to suspend the assembly. The episode was ominous because it indicated that Parliament was taking the Declaratory Act at its word; on no previous occasion had the British legislature intervened in the operation of the constitution in an American colony. (Such interventions, which were rare, had come from the crown.)

British intervention in colonial economic affairs occurred again when in 1773 Lord North's administration tried to rescue the East India Company from difficulties that had nothing to do with

2∞9 Boston Boys throwing tea into the harbour

At the Dec. 16, 1773, Boston Tea Party, Bostonians protested the Tea Tax by tossing some £10,000 worth of tea into the harbour. Edward Gooch/Hulton Archive/Getty Images

America. The Tea Act gave the company, which produced tea in India, a monopoly of distribution in the colonies. The company planned to sell its tea through its own agents, eliminating the system of sale by auction to independent merchants. By thus cutting the costs of middlemen, it hoped to undersell the widely purchased inferior smuggled tea. This plan naturally affected colonial merchants, and many colonists denounced the act as a plot to induce Americans to buy—and therefore pay the tax on—legally imported tea. Boston was not the only port to threaten to reject the casks of taxed tea, but its reply was the most dramatic—and provocative.

On Dec. 16, 1773, a party of Bostonians, thinly disguised as Mohawk Indians, boarded the ships at anchor and dumped some £10,000 worth of tea into the harbour, an event popularly known as the Boston Tea Party. British opinion was outraged, and America's friends in Parliament were immobilized. (American merchants in other cities were also disturbed. Property was property.) In the spring of 1774, with hardly any opposition, Parliament passed a series of measures designed to reduce Massachusetts to order and imperial discipline. The port of Boston was closed, and, in the Massachusetts Government Act, Parliament for the first time actually altered a colonial charter, substituting an appointive council for the elective one established in 1691 and conferring extensive powers on the governor and council. The famous town meeting, a forum for radical thinkers, was outlawed as a political body. To make matters worse, Parliament also passed the Quebec Act for the government of Canada. To the horror of pious New England Calvinists, the Roman Catholic religion was recognized for the French inhabitants. In addition, Upper Canada (i.e., the southern section) was joined to the Mississippi valley for purposes of administration, permanently blocking the prospect of American control of western settlement.

CHAPTER 2

THE CONTINENTAL CONGRESS

There was widespread agreement that this intervention in colonial government could threaten other provinces and could be countered only by collective action. After much intercolonial correspondence, a Continental Congress came into existence, meeting in Philadelphia in September 1774. Every colonial assembly except that of Georgia appointed and sent a delegation.

GETTING STARTED

The Virginia delegation's instructions were drafted by Thomas Jefferson and were later published as *A Summary View of the Rights of British America* (1774). Jefferson insisted on the autonomy of colonial legislative power and set forth a highly individualistic view of the basis of American rights. This belief that the American colonies and other members of the British Empire were distinct states united under the king and thus subject only to the king and not to Parliament was shared by several other delegates, notably James Wilson and John Adams, and strongly influenced the Congress.

George Washington (middle) *surrounded by members of the Continental Congress, hand-coloured lithograph by Currier & Ives, c. 1876.* Currier & Ives Collection, Library of Congress, Neg. No. LC-USZC2-3154

The Congress's first important decision was one on procedure: whether to vote by colony, each having one vote, or by wealth calculated on a ratio with population. The decision to vote by colony was made on practical grounds—neither wealth nor population could be satisfactorily ascertained—but it had important consequences. Individual colonies, no matter what their size, retained a degree of autonomy that translated immediately into the language and prerogatives of sovereignty. Under Massachusetts's

influence, the Congress next adopted the Suffolk Resolves, recently voted in Suffolk county, Mass., which for the first time put natural rights into the official colonial argument (hitherto all remonstrances had been based on common law and constitutional rights). Apart from this, however, the prevailing mood was cautious.

The Congress's aim was to put such pressure on the British government that it would redress all colonial grievances and restore the harmony that had once

Document: The Association of the Continental Congress (1774)

Most members of the First Continental Congress hoped that a commercial boycott would induce the British government to accede to their demands. On Oct. 20, 1774, the Congress voted for nonimportation, nonconsumption, and nonexportation, virtually cutting off trade with Britain. It was hoped that this economic maneuver would bring about the repeal of the Intolerable Acts. The nonintercourse agreement differed from previous colonial boycotts inasmuch as it derived from the people, working through committees, rather than from the merchants. The Continental Association was perhaps more successful politically than economically, because it helped to weld the colonies together into an American union.

We, His Majesty's most loyal subjects, the delegates of the several colonies of New Hampshire, Massachusetts Bay, Rhode Island, Connecticut, New York, New Jersey, Pennsylvania, the three lower counties of Newcastle, Kent, and Sussex on Delaware, Maryland, Virginia, North Carolina, and South Carolina, deputed to represent them in a Continental Congress, held in the city of Philadelphia, on the 5th day of September, 1774, avowing our allegiance to His Majesty, our affection and regard for our fellow subjects in Great Britain and elsewhere, affected with the deepest anxiety and most alarming apprehensions at those grievances and distresses, with which His Majesty's American subjects are oppressed; and having taken under our most serious deliberation the state of the whole continent, find that the present unhappy situation of our affairs is occasioned by a ruinous system of colony administration, adopted by the British Ministry about the year 1763, evidently calculated for enslaving these colonies and with them, the British empire.

In prosecution of which system, various acts of Parliament have been passed for raising a revenue in America; for depriving the American subjects, in many instances, of the constitutional trial by jury; exposing their lives to danger by directing a new and illegal trial beyond the seas for crimes alleged to have been committed in America. And in prosecution of the same system, several late, cruel, and oppressive acts have been passed respecting the town of Boston and the Massachusetts Bay, and also an act for extending the province of Quebec, so as to border on the western frontiers of these colonies, establishing an arbitrary government therein, and discouraging the settlement of British subjects in that wide-extended country; thus, by the influence of civil principles and ancient prejudices to dispose the inhabitants to act with hostility against the free Protestant colonies, whenever a wicked Ministry shall choose to direct them....

prevailed. The Congress thus adopted an Association that committed the colonies to a carefully phased plan of economic pressure, beginning with nonimportation, moving to nonconsumption, and finishing the following September (after the rice harvest had been exported) with nonexportation.

A few New England and Virginia delegates were looking toward independence, but the majority went home hoping that these steps, together with new appeals to the king and to the British people, would avert the need for any further such meetings. If these measures failed, however, a second Congress would convene the following spring.

DIVISION AND DISSENT

Behind the unity achieved by the Congress lay deep divisions in colonial society. In the mid-1760s upriver New York was disrupted by land riots, which also broke out in parts of New Jersey. Much worse disorder ravaged the backcountry of both North and South Carolina, where frontier people were left unprotected by legislatures that taxed them but in which they felt themselves unrepresented. A pitched battle at Alamance Creek in North Carolina in 1771 ended that rising, known as the Regulator Insurrection, and was followed by executions for treason. Although without such serious disorder, the cities also revealed acute social tensions and resentments of inequalities of economic opportunity and visible status. New York provincial politics were riven by intense rivalry between two great family-based factions, the DeLanceys, who benefited from royal government connections, and their rivals, the Livingstons. (The politics of the quarrel with Britain affected the domestic standing of these groups and eventually eclipsed the DeLanceys.) Another phenomenon was the rapid rise of dissenting religious sects, notably the Baptists. Although they carried no political program, the Baptist style of preaching suggested a strong undercurrent of social as well as religious dissent. There was no inherent unity to these disturbances, but many leaders of colonial society were reluctant to ally themselves with these disruptive elements even in protest against Britain. They were concerned about the domestic consequences of letting the protests take a revolutionary turn; power shared with these elements might never be recovered.

RADICAL ACTION OR LOYALISM

When British Gen. Thomas Gage sent a force from Boston to destroy American rebel military stores at Concord, Mass., fighting broke out between militia and British troops at Lexington and Concord on April 19, 1775. Reports of these clashes reached the Second Continental Congress, which met in Philadelphia in May. Although most colonial leaders still hoped for reconciliation with Britain, the news stirred the delegates to more radical action. Steps were taken to put the continent on a war footing. While a further appeal was addressed to the British people (mainly at Dickinson's insistence), the Congress raised an army, adopted a *Declaration of the Causes and Necessity of Taking Up Arms*, and appointed committees to

Document: The Necessity for Taking Up Arms (1775)

A Declaration...Setting Forth the Causes and Necessity of Their Taking Up Arms held out a hope of reconciliation with Britain, but at the same time approved the use of armed resistance to obtain recognition of the rights of the colonists. The final draft of the Declaration was the work of Thomas Jefferson and John Dickinson. Approved by the Second Continental Congress on July 6, 1775, the Declaration disavowed all thoughts of independence. The colonists claimed to be fighting a "ministerial army" and not the king, who they felt had been misled by evil counselors. The Americans promised to lay down their arms when the liberties they claimed as a birthright had been secured.

If it was possible for men who exercise their reason to believe that the Divine Author of our existence intended a part of the human race to hold an absolute property in and an unbounded power over others, marked out by His infinite goodness and wisdom, as the objects of a legal domination never rightfully resistible, however severe and oppressive, the inhabitants of these colonies might at least require from the Parliament of Great Britain some evidence that this dreadful authority over them has been granted to that body. But a reverence for our great Creator, principles of humanity, and the dictates of common sense must convince all those who reflect upon the subject that government was instituted to promote the welfare of mankind and ought to be administered for the attainment of that end.

The legislature of Great Britain, however, stimulated by an inordinate passion for a power not only unjustifiable but which they know to be peculiarly reprobated by the very constitution of that kingdom, and desperate of success in any mode of contest where regard should be had to truth, law, or right, have at length, deserting those, attempted to effect their cruel and impolitic purpose of enslaving these colonies by violence, and have thereby rendered it necessary for us to close with their last appeal from reason to arms. Yet, however blinded that assembly may be by their intemperate rage for unlimited domination so to slight justice and the opinion of mankind, we esteem ourselves bound, by obligations of respect to the rest of the world, to make known the justice of our cause....

deal with domestic supply and foreign affairs.

In August 1775 the king declared a state of rebellion; by the end of the year, all colonial trade had been banned. Even yet, Gen. George Washington, commander of the Continental Army, still referred to the British troops as "ministerial" forces, indicating a civil war, not a war looking to separate national identity.

Then in January 1776 the publication of Thomas Paine's irreverent pamphlet *Common Sense* abruptly shattered this hopeful complacency and put independence on the agenda. Paine's eloquent, direct language spoke people's unspoken thoughts; no pamphlet had

Thomas Paine. Library of Congress Prints and Photographs Division

Document: Thomas Paine: Plain Arguments for Independence [from *Common Sense*] (1776)

As the American Revolution progressed, the attitude of the British authorities made it apparent that no concessions could be expected. The idea of complete independence, which was beginning to win more and more support, was the subject of discussion in a pamphlet written by newly arrived English immigrant Thomas Paine. Published in January 1776, Common Sense *pressed the argument for independence in logically compelling terms. Paine's reasoning convinced George Washington, who wrote to Joseph Reed of Pennsylvania on Jan. 31, 1776: "A few more of such flaming arguments, as were exhibited at Falmouth and Norfolk, added to the sound doctrine and unanswerable reasoning contained in the pamphlet Common Sense, will not leave numbers at a loss to decide upon the propriety of a separation."*

In the following pages I offer nothing more than simple facts, plain arguments, and common sense; and have no other preliminaries to settle with the reader than that he will divest himself of prejudice and prepossession, and suffer his reason and his feelings to determine for themselves; that he will put *on*, or rather that he will not put *off*, the true character of a man, and generously enlarge his views beyond the present day.

Volumes have been written on the subject of the struggle between England and America. Men of all ranks have embarked in the controversy, from different motives and with various designs; but all have been ineffectual, and the period of debate is closed. Arms, as the last resource, must decide the contest; the appeal was the choice of the king, and the continent has accepted the challenge....

ever made such an impact on colonial opinion.

While the Congress negotiated urgently, but secretly, for a French alliance, power struggles erupted in provinces where conservatives still hoped for relief. The only form relief could take, however, was British concessions; as public opinion hardened in Britain, where a general election in November 1774 had returned a strong majority for Lord North, the hope for reconciliation faded. In the face of British intransigence, men committed to their definition of colonial rights were left with no alternative, and the substantial portion of colonists—about one-third according to John Adams, although contemporary historians believe the number to have been much smaller—who preferred loyalty to the crown, with all its disadvantages, were localized and outflanked. Where the British armies massed, they found plenty of loyalist support, but, when they moved on, they left the loyalists feeble and exposed.

Image of the Declaration of Independence (1776) taken from an engraving made by printer William J. Stone in 1823. National Archives, Washington, D.C.

Document: The Declaration of Independence (1776)

The Declaration of Independence was formally adopted by the delegates to the Second Continental Congress, meeting in Philadelphia, on July 4, 1776. Two days earlier, a resolution had been passed which said "that these United Colonies are, and of right ought to be, free and independent States, that they are absolved from all allegiance to the British Crown, and that all political connection between them and the state of Great Britain is and ought to be totally dissolved." The introduction on June 7 of this resolution, by Richard Henry Lee of Virginia, had been followed by the appointment of a committee to draft a statement declaring the reasons for the impending separation. Of the members of this committee, which included Thomas Jefferson, John Adams, Benjamin Franklin, Roger Sherman, and Robert Livingston, it was Jefferson who prepared the draft, submitting it to the others for consideration. Minor changes in Jefferson's draft were suggested by Adams and Franklin. Some further alterations were made after it was presented to the Congress on June 28. The final words, however, were still largely those of Jefferson. At its passage it was signed only by John Hancock, the presiding officer. Four days later the Declaration of Independence was read aloud in the city of Philadelphia at what later became Independence Square. Copies were made, sent to the legislatures of the colonies, and published throughout the country. The Declaration was not signed by the other members of the Congress until August 2, when a copy engrossed on parchment was witnessed with their names.

When, in the course of human events, it becomes necessary for one people to dissolve the political bands which have connected them with another, and to assume, among the powers of the earth, the separate and equal station to which the laws of nature and of nature's God entitle them, a decent respect to the opinions of mankind requires that they should declare the causes which impel them to the separation.

We hold these truths to be self-evident, that all men are created equal, that they are endowed by their Creator with certain unalienable rights, that among these are life, liberty, and the pursuit of happiness. That, to secure these rights, governments are instituted among men, deriving their just powers from the consent of the governed. That, whenever any form of government becomes destructive of these ends, it is the right of the people to alter or to abolish it, and to institute new government, laying its foundation on such principles, and organizing its powers in such form, as to them shall seem most likely to effect their safety and happiness.

Prudence, indeed, will dictate that governments long established should not be changed for light and transient causes; and, accordingly, all experience has shown, that mankind are more disposed to suffer, while evils are sufferable, than to right themselves by abolishing the forms to which they are accustomed.

But, when a long train of abuses and usurpations, pursuing invariably the same object, evinces a design to reduce them under absolute despotism, it is their right, it is their duty, to throw off such government, and to provide new guards for their future security. Such has been the patient sufferance of these colonies; and such is now the necessity which constrains them to alter their former systems of government. The history of the present King of Great Britain is a history of repeated injuries and usurpations, all having in direct object the establishment of an absolute tyranny over these states. To prove this, let facts be submitted to a candid world....

The most dramatic internal revolution occurred in Pennsylvania, where a strong radical party, based mainly in Philadelphia but with allies in the country, seized power in the course of the controversy over independence itself. Opinion for independence swept the colonies in the spring of 1776. The Congress recommended that colonies form their own governments and assigned a committee to draft a declaration of independence.

This document, written by Thomas Jefferson but revised in committee, consisted of two parts. The preamble set the claims of the United States on a basis of natural rights, with a dedication to the principle of equality; the second was a long list of grievances against the crown—not Parliament now, because the argument was that Parliament had no lawful power in the colonies. On July 2 the Congress itself voted for independence; on July 4 it adopted the Declaration of Independence.

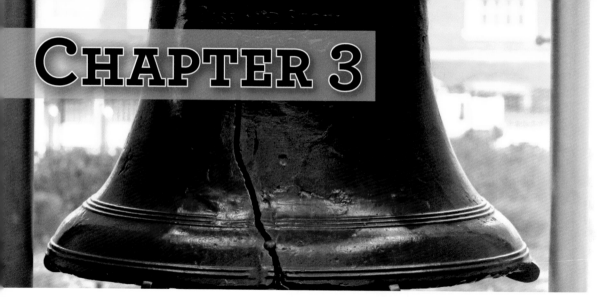

Chapter 3

The American Revolutionary War

The American Revolutionary War thus began as a civil conflict within the British Empire over colonial affairs, but, with America being joined by France in 1778, Spain in 1779, and the Netherlands in 1780, it became an international war. On land the Americans assembled both state militias and the Continental (national) Army, with approximately 20,000 men, mostly farmers, fighting at any given time. By contrast, the British army was composed of reliable and well-trained professionals, numbering about 42,000 regulars, supplemented by about 30,000 German (Hessian) mercenaries.

FROM LEXINGTON TO YORKTOWN

After the fighting at Lexington and Concord that began the war, rebel forces began a siege of Boston that ended when the American Gen. Henry Knox arrived with artillery captured from Fort Ticonderoga, forcing Gen. William Howe, Gage's replacement, to evacuate Boston on March 17, 1776. An American force under Gen. Richard Montgomery invaded

Canada in the fall of 1775, captured Montreal, and launched an unsuccessful attack on Quebec, in which Montgomery was killed. The Americans maintained a siege on the city until the arrival of British reinforcements in the spring and then retreated to Fort Ticonderoga.

The British government sent Howe's brother, Richard, Adm. Lord Howe, with a large fleet to join his brother in New York, authorizing them to treat with the Americans and assure them pardon should they submit. When the Americans refused this offer of peace, General Howe landed on Long Island and on August 27 defeated the army led by Washington, who retreated into Manhattan. Howe drew him north, defeated his army at Chatterton Hill near White Plains on October 28, and then stormed the garrison Washington had left behind on Manhattan, seizing prisoners and supplies. Lord Charles Cornwallis, having taken Washington's other garrison at Fort Lee, drove the American army across New Jersey to the western bank of the Delaware River and then quartered his troops for the winter at outposts in New Jersey. On Christmas night Washington stealthily crossed the Delaware and attacked Cornwallis's garrison at Trenton, taking nearly 1,000 prisoners. Though Cornwallis soon recaptured Trenton, Washington escaped and went on to defeat British reinforcements at Princeton. Washington's Trenton-Princeton campaign roused the new country and kept the struggle for independence alive.

Gen. William Howe, 1778. Library of Congress, Washington, D.C.

In 1777 a British army under Gen. John Burgoyne moved south from Canada with Albany, N.Y., as its goal. Burgoyne captured Fort Ticonderoga on July 5, but, as he approached Albany, he was twice defeated by an American force led by Generals Horatio Gates and Benedict Arnold, and on Oct. 17, 1777, at Saratoga, he was forced to surrender his army. Earlier that fall Howe had sailed from New York to Chesapeake Bay, and once ashore he had defeated Washington's forces at Brandywine Creek on September 11 and occupied the American capital of Philadelphia on September 25.

Document: George Washington: On the Organization of the Army (1778)

After the Battle of Bunker Hill, Gen. George Washington was put in command of the Continental Army in Massachusetts. His task was to transform a disorganized mob of patriotic recruits into a disciplined army, all the while fighting a war. By early 1778, several deficiencies in the military establishment had become apparent. Discipline, officer status, and short-term enlistments were among the problems that caused Washington to appeal to Congress for a reorganization of the army. The following communication was addressed to a committee of Congress on Jan. 28, 1778, while the army was in camp at Valley Forge. It was issued under Washington's name, but it was written by Alexander Hamilton, who was Washington's confidential aide from 1777 to 1781.

The numerous defects in our present military establishment, rendering many reformations and many new arrangements absolutely necessary, and Congress having been pleased to appoint you a committee, in concert with me, to make and recommend such as shall appear eligible, in pursuance of the various objects expressed in the resolution, for that purpose; I have, in the following sheets, briefly delivered my sentiments upon such of them as appeared to me most essential, so far as observation has suggested and leisure permitted. These are submitted to consideration, and I shall be happy, if they are found conducive to remedying the evils and inconveniences we are now subject to, and putting the army upon a more respectable footing. Something must be done; important alterations must be made; necessity requires that our resources should be enlarged and our system improved, for without it, if the dissolution of the army should not be the consequence, at least its operations must be feeble, languid, and ineffectual.

As I consider a proper and satisfactory provision for officers as the basis of every other arrangement and regulation necessary to be made (since without officers no army can exist) and unless some measures be devised to place those officers in a more desirable condition, few of them would be able, if willing, to continue in it. ...

After a mildly successful attack at Germantown, Pa., on October 4, Washington quartered his 11,000 troops for the winter at Valley Forge, Pa. Though the conditions at Valley Forge were bleak and food was scarce, a Prussian officer, Baron Friedrich Wilhelm von Steuben, was able to give the American troops valuable training in maneuvers and in the more efficient use of their weapons. Von Steuben's aid contributed greatly to Washington's success at Monmouth (now Freehold), N.J., on June 28, 1778. After that battle British forces in the north remained chiefly in and around the city of New York.

While the French had been secretly furnishing financial and material aid to the Americans since 1776, in 1778 they began to prepare fleets and armies and in June finally declared war on Britain. With action in the north largely a stalemate, their primary contribution was in the south, where they participated in such undertakings as the siege of British-held Savannah and the decisive siege of Yorktown. Cornwallis destroyed an army under Gates at Camden, S.C., on Aug. 16, 1780, but suffered heavy setbacks at Kings Mountain, S.C., on October 7 and at Cowpens, S.C., on Jan. 17, 1781. After Cornwallis won a costly victory at Guilford Courthouse, N.C., on March 15, 1781, he entered Virginia to join other British forces there, setting up a base at Yorktown. Washington's army and a force under the French Count de Rochambeau placed Yorktown under siege, and Cornwallis surrendered his army of more than 7,000 men on Oct. 19, 1781.

Cow representing British commerce being milked and dehorned by France, Spain, Holland, and the United States while the British lion sleeps, during the American Revolutionary War. Library of Congress, Washington, D.C.

Siege of Yorktown

The Siege of Yorktown (Sept. 28–Oct. 19, 1781) was a joint Franco-American land and sea campaign that entrapped a major British army on a peninsula at Yorktown, Va., and forced its surrender. The siege virtually ended military operations in the American Revolution.

After a series of reverses and the depletion of his forces' strength, the British commander in the southern colonies, Gen. Lord Cornwallis, moved his army from Wilmington, N.C., eastward to Petersburg, Va., on the Atlantic coast, in May 1781. Cornwallis had about 7,500 men and was confronted in the region by only about 4,500 American troops under the marquis de Lafayette, Gen. Anthony Wayne, and Frederick William, Freiherr (baron) von Steuben. To maintain his seaborne lines of communication with the main British army of Gen. Henry Clinton in New York City, Cornwallis then retreated through Virginia, first to Richmond, next to Williamsburg, and finally, near the end of July, to Yorktown and the adjacent promontory of Gloucester, both of which he proceeded to fortify.

The American commander in chief, Gen. George Washington, ordered Lafayette to block Cornwallis's possible escape from Yorktown by land. In the meantime Washington's 2,500 Continental troops in New York were joined by 4,000 French troops under the comte de Rochambeau. This combined allied force left a screen of troops facing Clinton's forces in New York while the main Franco-American force, beginning on August 21, undertook a rapid march southward to the head of Chesapeake Bay, where it linked up with a French fleet of 24 ships under the comte de Grasse. This fleet had arrived from the West Indies and was maintaining a sea blockade of Cornwallis's army. Cornwallis's army waited in vain for rescue or reinforcements from the British navy while de Grasse's fleet transported Washington's troops southward to Williamsburg, Va., whence they joined Lafayette's forces in the siege of Yorktown. Washington was thus vindicated in his hopes of entrapping Cornwallis on the Yorktown Peninsula.

Meanwhile, a smaller British fleet under Adm. Thomas Graves was unable to counter French naval superiority at the Battle of Virginia Capes and felt forced to return to New York. A British rescue fleet, two-thirds the size of the French, set out for Virginia on October 17 with some 7,000 British troops, but it was too late. Throughout early October Washington's 14,000 Franco-American troops steadily overcame the British army's fortified positions at Yorktown. Surrounded, outgunned, and running low on food, Cornwallis surrendered his entire army on October 19. The total number of British prisoners taken was about 8,000, along with about 240 guns. Casualties on both sides were relatively light. The victory at Yorktown ended fighting in the Revolution and virtually assured success to the American cause.

Thereafter, land action in America died out, though war continued on the high seas. Although a Continental Navy was created in 1775, the American sea effort lapsed largely into privateering, and after 1780 the war at sea was fought chiefly between Britain and America's European allies. Still, American

Etching showing atrocities against Loyalists. Library of Congress, Washington, D.C.

privateers swarmed around the British Isles, and by the end of the war they had captured 1,500 British merchant ships and 12,000 sailors. After 1780 Spain and the Netherlands were able to control much of the water around the British Isles, thus keeping the bulk of British naval forces tied down in Europe.

TREATY OF PARIS

The military verdict in North America was reflected in the preliminary Anglo-American peace treaty of 1782, which was included in the Treaty of Paris

of 1783. Franklin, John Adams, John Jay, and Henry Laurens served as the American commissioners. By its terms Britain recognized the independence of the United States with generous boundaries, including the Mississippi River on the west. Britain retained Canada but ceded East and West Florida to Spain. Provisions were inserted calling for the payment of American private debts to British citizens, for American access to the Newfoundland fisheries, and for a recommendation by the Continental Congress to the states in favour of fair treatment of the loyalists.

Most of the loyalists remained in the new country; however, perhaps as many as 80,000 Tories migrated to Canada, England, and the British West Indies. Many of these had served as British soldiers, and many had been banished by the American states. The loyalists were harshly treated as dangerous enemies by the American states during the war and immediately afterward. They were commonly deprived of civil rights, often fined, and frequently relieved of their property.

The more conspicuous were usually banished upon pain of death. The British government compensated more than 4,000 of the exiles for property losses, paying out almost £3.3 million. It also gave them land grants, pensions, and appointments to enable them to reestablish themselves. The less ardent and more cautious Tories, staying in the United States, accepted the separation from Britain as final and, after the passage of a generation, could not be distinguished from the patriots.

CHAPTER 4

FOUNDATIONS OF THE AMERICAN REPUBLIC

It had been far from certain that the Americans could fight a successful war against the might of Britain. The scattered colonies had little inherent unity; their experience of collective action was limited; an army had to be created and maintained; they had no common institutions other than the Continental Congress; and they had almost no experience of continental public finance. The Americans could not have hoped to win the war without French help, and the French monarchy—whose interests were anti-British but not pro-American—had waited watchfully to see what the Americans could do in the field. Although the French began supplying arms, clothing, and loans surreptitiously soon after the Americans declared independence, it was not until 1778 that a formal alliance was forged.

SOURCES OF STRENGTH

Most of these problems lasted beyond the achievement of independence and continued to vex American politics for many years, even for generations. Meanwhile, however, the colonies had valuable, though less visible, sources of strength. Practically all farmers had their own arms and could form into militia companies overnight. More fundamentally, Americans had for many years been receiving basically the same information, mainly from the English press, reprinted in identical form in colonial newspapers. The effect of this was to form a singularly wide body of agreed opinion about major public issues. Another force of incalculable importance was the fact that for several generations Americans had to a large extent been governing themselves through elected assemblies, which in turn had developed sophisticated experience in committee politics.

This factor of "institutional memory" was of great importance in the forming of a mentality of self-government. Men became attached to their habitual ways, especially when these were habitual ways of running their own affairs, and these habits formed the basis of an ideology just as pervasive and important to the people concerned as republican theories published in Britain and the European continent. Moreover, colonial self-government seemed, from a colonial point of view, to be continuous and consistent with the principles of English government—principles for which Parliament had fought the Civil Wars in the mid-17th century and which colonists believed to have been reestablished by the Glorious Revolution of 1688–89. It was equally important that experience of self-government had taught colonial leaders how to get things done. When the Continental Congress met in 1774, members did not have to debate procedure (except on voting); they already knew it. Finally, the Congress's authority was rooted in traditions of legitimacy. The old election laws were used. Voters could transfer their allegiance with minimal difficulty from the dying colonial assemblies to the new assemblies and conventions of the states.

PROBLEMS BEFORE THE SECOND CONTINENTAL CONGRESS

When the Second Continental Congress assembled in Philadelphia in May 1775, revolution was not a certainty. The Congress had to prepare for that contingency nevertheless and thus was confronted by two parallel sets of problems. The first was how to organize for war; the second, which proved less urgent but could not be set aside forever, was how to define the legal relationship between the Congress and the states.

In June 1775, in addition to appointing Washington (who had made a point of turning up in uniform) commander in chief, the Congress provided for the enlistment of an army. It then turned to the vexatious problems of finance. An aversion to taxation being one of the unities of American sentiment, the

Congress began by trying to raise a domestic loan. It did not have much success, however, for the excellent reason that the outcome of the operation appeared highly dubious. At the same time, authority was taken for issuing a paper currency. This proved to be the most important method of domestic war finance, and, as the war years passed, Congress resorted to issuing more and more Continental currency, which depreciated rapidly and had to compete with currencies issued by state governments. (People were inclined to prefer local currencies.) The Continental Army was a further source of a form of currency because its commission agents issued certificates in exchange for goods. These certificates bore an official promise of redemption and could be used in personal transactions. Loans raised overseas, notably in France and the Netherlands, were another important source of revenue.

In 1780 Congress decided to call in all former issues of currency and replace them with a new issue on a 40-to-1 ratio. The Philadelphia merchant Robert Morris, who was appointed superintendent of finance in 1781 and came to be known as "the Financier," guided the United States through its complex fiscal difficulties. Morris's personal finances were inextricably tangled up with those of the country, and he became the object of much hostile comment, but he also used his own resources to secure urgently needed loans from abroad. In 1781 Morris secured a charter for the first Bank of North America, an institution that owed much to the example of the Bank of England. Although the bank was attacked by radical egalitarians as an unrepublican manifestation of privilege, it gave the United States a firmer financial foundation.

The problem of financing and organizing the war sometimes overlapped with Congress's other major problem, that of defining its relations with the states. The Congress, being only an association of states, had no power to tax individuals. The Articles of Confederation, a plan of government organization adopted and put into practice by Congress in 1777, although not officially ratified by all the states until 1781, gave Congress the right to make requisitions on the states proportionate to their ability to pay. The states in turn had to raise these sums by their own domestic powers to tax, a method that state legislators looking for reelection were reluctant to employ. The result was that many states were constantly in heavy arrears, and, particularly after the urgency of the war years had subsided, the Congress's ability to meet expenses and repay its war debts was crippled.

The Congress lacked power to enforce its requisitions and fell badly behind in repaying its wartime creditors. When individual states (Maryland as early as 1782, Pennsylvania in 1785) passed legislation providing for repayment of the debt owed to their own

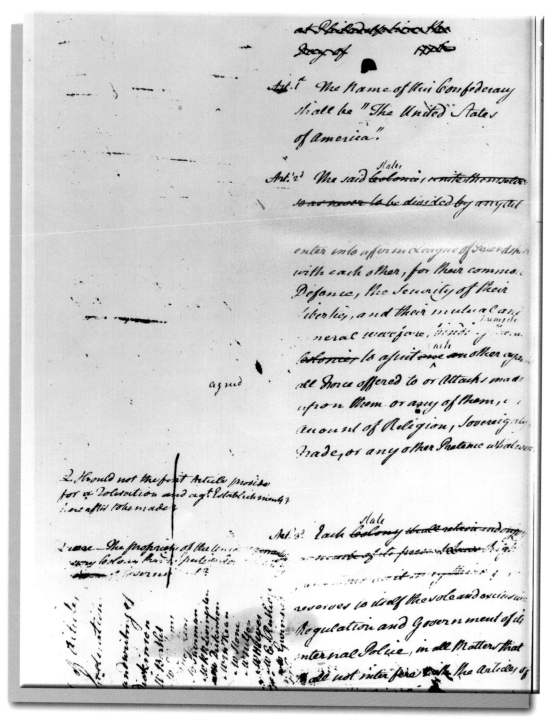

John Dickinson's draft of the Articles of Confederation. National Archives, Washington, D.C.

citizens by the Continental Congress, one of the reasons for the Congress's existence had begun to crumble. Two attempts were made to get the states to agree to grant the Congress the power it needed to raise revenue by levying an impost on imports. Each failed for want of unanimous consent. Essentially,

Document: The Articles of Confederation (1781)

On June 7, 1776, Richard Henry Lee moved that Congress appoint a committee to draw up articles of confederation among the several states—as they would soon be if his resolution for independence was adopted. One member of each state was chosen for this committee, which on July 12 presented a plan of union drafted by John Dickinson of Pennsylvania. Dickinson's plan was much debated and not until November 1777 was it adopted in greatly revised form. It did not go into effect until 1781, because the ratification of all the states was required for its adoption. It has become as common to defend the Articles as formerly it was to malign them. Certainly they did not create, nor could any form of government have easily cured, the postwar economic depression that beset the former colonies. The trouble was that the Confederation which the Articles established was not a federation, though it was a good deal more, at least on paper, than a mere league between the states. It had no control over taxation and trade, it lacked both a federal executive and a federal judiciary, and it was entirely without sanctions by which the Congress could enforce its will. The result was that relations within the Confederation were essentially international, while at the same time the states were without the resources to function as independent sovereignties. Such an arrangement could not last indefinitely; in fact, it was superseded within eight years by the government set up by the Constitution.

Article I. The style of this confederacy shall be "The United States of America."

Article II. Each state retains its sovereignty, freedom, and independence, and every power, jurisdiction, and right which is not by this confederation expressly delegated to the United States in Congress assembled.

Article III. The said states hereby severally enter into a firm league of friendship with each other, for their common defense, the security of their liberties, and their mutual and general welfare, binding themselves to assist each other against all force offered to, or attacks made upon them, or any of them, on account of religion, sovereignty, trade, or any other pretense whatever.

Article IV. The better to secure and perpetuate mutual friendship and intercourse among the people of the different states in this union, the free inhabitants of each of these states, paupers, vagabonds, and fugitives from justice excepted, shall be entitled to all privileges and immunities of free citizens in the several states; and the people of each state shall have free ingress and regress to and from any other state and shall enjoy therein all the privileges of trade and commerce, subject to the same duties, impositions, and restrictions as the inhabitants thereof respectively, provided that such restrictions shall not extend so far as to prevent the removal of property imported into any state, to any other state of which the owner is an inhabitant; provided also that no imposition, duties, or restriction shall be laid by any state on the property of the United States, or either of them....

an impost would have been collected at ports, which belonged to individual states—there was no "national" territory—and therefore cut across the concept of state sovereignty. Agreement was nearly obtained on each occasion, and, if it had been, the Constitutional Convention might never have been called. But the failure sharply pointed up the weakness of the Congress and of the union between the states under the Articles of Confederation.

The Articles of Confederation reflected strong preconceptions of state sovereignty. Article II expressly reserved sovereignty to the states individually, and another article even envisaged the possibility that one state might go to war without the others. Fundamental revisions could be made only with unanimous consent, because the Articles represented a treaty between sovereigns, not the creation of a new nation-state. Other major revisions required the consent of nine states. Yet state sovereignty principles rested on artificial foundations. The states could never have achieved independence on their own, and in fact the Congress had taken the first step both in recommending that the states form their own governments and in declaring their collective independence. Most important of its domestic responsibilities, by 1787 the Congress had enacted several ordinances establishing procedures for incorporating new territories. (It had been conflicts over western land

claims that had held up ratification of the Articles. Eventually the states with western claims, principally New York and Virginia, ceded them to the United States.) The Northwest Ordinance of 1787 provided for the phased settlement and government of territories in the Ohio valley, leading to eventual admission as new states. It also excluded the introduction of slavery—though it did not exclude the retention of existing slaves.

The states had constantly looked to the Congress for leadership in the difficulties of war; now that the danger was past, however, disunity began to threaten to turn into disintegration. The Congress was largely discredited in the eyes of a wide range of influential men, representing both old and new interests. The states were setting up their own tariff barriers against each other and quarreling among themselves; virtual war had broken out between competing settlers from Pennsylvania and Connecticut claiming the same lands. By 1786, well-informed men were discussing a probable breakup of the confederation into three or more new groups, which could have led to wars between the American republics.

STATE POLITICS

The problems of forming a new government affected the states individually as well as in confederation. Most of them established their own

Document: The Constitution of Vermont (1777)

The work of state constitution-making progressed rapidly in the midst of the war. By July of 1777, all the states but three had constitutions of their own devising. Vermont's first constitution, adopted July 8, 1777, was a copy of the democratic constitution of Pennsylvania. Vermont was not at this time recognized as a separate state by the rest of the colonies; its territory was claimed by both New Hampshire and New York. Thus the preamble is a declaration of independence from New York. The body of the constitution also contained provisions regarding civil liberties and expressly forbade the importation of slaves.

Whereas all government ought to be instituted and supported for the security and protection of the community, as such, and to enable the individuals who compose it to enjoy their natural rights, and other blessings which the Author of existence has bestowed upon man; and whenever those great ends of government are not obtained, the people have a right, by common consent, to change it, and take such measures as to them may appear necessary to promote their safety and happiness; And whereas the inhabitants of this state have (in consideration of protection only) heretofore acknowledged allegiance to the King of Great Britain, and the said King has not only withdrawn that protection, but commenced, and still continues to carry on, with unabated vengeance, a most cruel and unjust war against them; employing therein not only the troops of Great Britain, but foreign mercenaries, savages and slaves, for the avowed purpose of reducing them to a total and abject submission to the despotic domination of the British Parliament, with many other acts of tyranny (more fully set forth in the declaration of Congress) whereby all allegiance and fealty to the said King and his successors are dissolved and at an end, and all power and authority derived from him ceased in the American colonies....

constitutions—formulated either in conventions or in the existing assemblies. The most democratic of these constitutions was the product of a virtual revolution in Pennsylvania, where a highly organized radical party seized the opportunity of the revolutionary crisis to gain power. Suffrage was put on a taxpayer basis, with nearly all adult males paying some tax; representation was reformed to bring in the populations of western counties; and a single-chamber legislature was established. An oath of loyalty to the constitution for some time excluded political opponents and particularly Quakers (who could not take oaths) from participation. The constitutions of the other states reflected the firm political ascendancy of the traditional ruling elite. Power ascended from a broad base in the elective franchise and representation through a narrowing hierarchy of offices restricted by property qualifications. State governors had in some cases to be men of great wealth. Senators were either wealthy or elected by the wealthy sector of the electorate. (These conditions were not invariable; Virginia, which had a powerful landed elite, dispensed with such restrictions.) Several states retained religious qualifications for office. The separation of church and state was not a popular concept, and minorities such as Baptists and Quakers were subjected to indignities that amounted in some places (notably Massachusetts and Connecticut) to forms of persecution.

Elite power provided a lever for one of the most significant transformations of the era, one that took place almost without being either noticed or intended. This was the acceptance of the principle of giving representation in legislative bodies in proportion to population. It was made not only possible but attractive when the larger aggregations of population broadly coincided with the highest concentrations of property: great merchants and landowners from populous areas could continue to exert political ascendancy so long as they retained some sort of hold on the political process. The principle reemerged to dominate the distribution of voters in the House of Representatives and in the electoral college under the new federal Constitution.

Relatively conservative constitutions did little to stem a tide of increasingly democratic politics. The old elites had to wrestle with new political forces (and in the process they learned how to organize in the new regime). Executive

power was weakened. Many elections were held annually, and terms were limited. Legislatures quickly admitted new representatives from recent settlements, many with little previous political experience.

The new state governments, moreover, had to tackle major issues that affected all classes. The needs of public finance led to emissions of paper money. In several states these were resumed after the war, and, because they tended (though not invariably) to depreciate, they led directly to fierce controversies. The treatment of loyalists was also a theme of intense political dispute after the war. Despite the protests of men such as Alexander Hamilton, who urged restoration of property and rights, in many states loyalists were driven out and their estates seized and redistributed in forms of auction, providing opportunities for speculation rather than personal occupation. Many states were depressed economically. In Massachusetts, which remained under orthodox control, stiff taxation under conditions of postwar depression trapped many farmers into debt. Unable to meet their obligations, they rose late in 1786 under a Revolutionary War officer, Capt. Daniel Shays, in a movement to prevent the court sessions. Shays's Rebellion was crushed early in 1787 by an army raised in the state.

The action caused only a few casualties, but the episode sent a shiver of fear throughout the country's

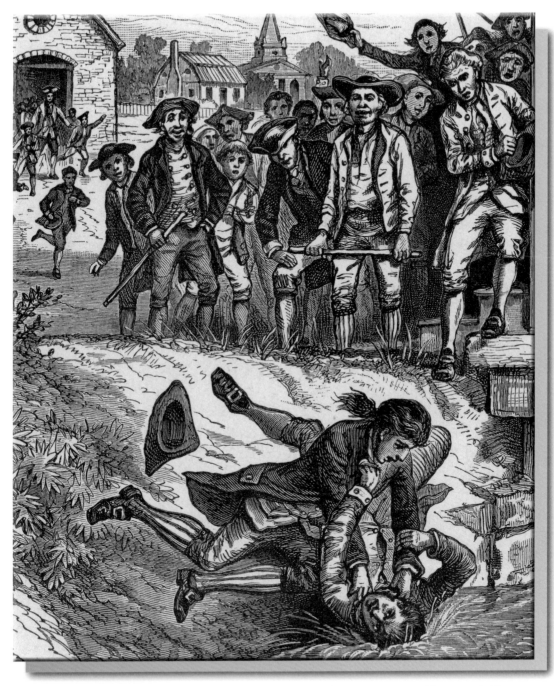

Fighting during Shays's Rebellion, an uprising in Massachusetts instigated by Daniel Shays in opposition to high taxes and severe economic conditions. Hulton Archive/Getty Images

Document: Daniel Gray: The Causes of Shays's Rebellion (1786)

Daniel Gray, as chairman of a committee of rebels protesting the Massachusetts debtors' plight, wrote an address to the people of Hampshire County. In the address Gray enumerated the causes for the riots that were staged under the leadership of Daniel Shays.

We have thought proper to inform you of some of the principal causes of the late risings of the people and also of their present movements, viz.:

- The present expensive mode of collecting debts, which by reason of the great scarcity of cash will of necessity fill our jails with unhappy debtors, and thereby a reputable body of people rendered incapable of being serviceable either to themselves or the community.
- The monies raised by impost and excise being appropriated to discharge the interest of governmental securities, and not the foreign debt, when these securities are not subject to taxation.
- A suspension of the writ of habeas corpus, by which those persons who have stepped forth to assert and maintain the rights of the people are liable to be taken and conveyed even to the most distant part of the commonwealth, and thereby subjected to an unjust punishment.
- The unlimited power granted to justices of the peace, and sheriffs, deputy sheriffs, and constables by the Riot Act, indemnifying them to the prosecution thereof; when perhaps wholly actuated from a principle of revenge, hatred, and envy.

Furthermore, be assured that this body, now at arms, depise the idea of being instigated by British emissaries, which is so strenuously propagated by the enemies of our liberties; and also wish the most proper and speedy measures may be taken to discharge both our foreign and domestic debt.

George R. Minot, *The History of the Insurrections in Massachusetts in the Year 1786 and the Rebellion Consequent Thereon,* 2nd edition, Boston, 1810, pp. 82–83.

propertied classes. It also seemed to justify the classical thesis that republics were unstable. It thus provided a potent stimulus to state legislatures to send delegates to the convention called (following a preliminary meeting in Annapolis) to meet at Philadelphia to revise the Articles of Confederation.

CHAPTER 5

THE CONSTITUTIONAL CONVENTION

Shay's Rebellion thus provided a potent stimulus to state legislatures to send delegates to the convention called (following a preliminary meeting in Annapolis) to revise the Articles of Confederation. That convention met at the Pennsylvania State House in Philadelphia from May 25–September 17, 1787. All the states except Rhode Island sent delegates. Of the 74 deputies chosen by the state legislatures, only 55 took part in the proceedings; of these, 39 signed the Constitution. The delegates included many of the leading figures of the period. Among them were George Washington, who was elected to preside, James Madison, Benjamin Franklin, James Wilson, John Rutledge, Charles Pinckney, Oliver Ellsworth, and Gouverneur Morris.

THE INFLUENCE OF THE VIRGINIA AND NEW JERSEY PLANS

The Philadelphia Convention, which met in May 1787, was officially called for by the old Congress solely to remedy defects in the Articles of Confederation. But the Virginia Plan presented by the Virginia delegates went beyond revision and boldly proposed to introduce a new, national government in place of the existing confederation. The convention thus immediately faced the question of whether the United States was to be a country in the modern sense or would continue as a weak federation of autonomous and equal states represented in a single chamber, which was the principle embodied in the New Jersey Plan presented by several small states. This decision was effectively made when a compromise plan for a bicameral legislature—one house with representation based on population and one with equal representation for all states—was approved in mid-July. Though neither plan prevailed, the new national government in its final form was endowed with broad powers that made it indisputably national and superior.

The Constitution, as it emerged after a summer of debate, embodied a much stronger principle of separation of powers than was generally to be found in the state constitutions. The chief executive was to be a single figure (a composite executive was discussed and rejected) and was to be elected by an electoral college, meeting in the states. This followed much debate over the Virginia Plan's preference for legislative election. The principal control on the chief executive, or president, against violation of the Constitution was the rather remote threat of impeachment (to which James Madison attached great importance). The Virginia Plan's proposal that representation be proportional to population in both houses was severely modified by the retention of equal representation for each state in the Senate. But the question of whether to count slaves in the population was abrasive. After some contention, antislavery forces gave way to a compromise by which three-fifths of the slaves would be counted as population for purposes of representation (and direct taxation). Slave states would thus be perpetually overrepresented in national politics; provision was also added for a law permitting the recapture of fugitive slaves, though in deference to republican scruples the word *slaves* was not used.

BALANCING POWER

Contemporary theory expected the legislature to be the most powerful branch of government. Thus, to balance the system, the executive was given a veto, and a judicial system with powers of review was established. It was also implicit in the structure that the new federal judiciary would have power to veto any state laws that conflicted either with the Constitution or with federal statutes. States were forbidden to pass laws impairing obligations of contract—a measure aimed at encouraging capital—and the Congress could pass no ex post facto law.

Sidebar: The Founding Fathers and Slavery

SLAVEHOLDERS AMONG PROMINENT FOUNDING FATHERS

SLAVEHOLDERS[1]		NONSLAVEHOLDERS	
FOUNDING FATHER	STATE	FOUNDING FATHER	STATE
Charles Carroll	Maryland	John Adams	Massachusetts
Samuel Chase	Maryland	Samuel Adams	Massachusetts
Benjamin Franklin	Pennsylvania	Oliver Ellsworth	Connecticut
Button Gwinnett	Georgia	Alexander Hamilton	New York
John Hancock	Massachusetts	Robert Treat Paine	Massachusetts
Patrick Henry	Virginia	Thomas Paine	Pennsylvania
John Jay	New York	Roger Sherman	Connecticut
Thomas Jefferson	Virginia		
Richard Henry Lee	Virginia		
James Madison	Virginia		
Charles Cotesworth Pinckney	South Carolina		
Benjamin Rush	Pennsylvania		
Edward Rutledge	South Carolina		
George Washington	Virginia		

[1]Held slaves at some point in time.

Although many of the Founding Fathers acknowledged that slavery violated the core American Revolutionary ideal of liberty, their simultaneous commitment to private property rights, principles of limited government, and intersectional harmony prevented them from making a bold move against slavery. The considerable investment of Southern Founders in slave-based staple agriculture, combined with their deep-seated racial prejudice, posed additional obstacles to emancipation.

In his initial draft of the Declaration of Independence, Thomas Jefferson condemned the injustice of the slave trade and, by implication, slavery, but he also blamed the presence of enslaved Africans in North America on avaricious British colonial policies. Jefferson thus acknowledged that slavery violated the natural rights of the enslaved, while at the same time he absolved Americans of any responsibility for owning slaves themselves. The Continental Congress apparently rejected the tortured logic of this passage by deleting it from the final document, but this decision also signaled the Founders' commitment to subordinating the controversial issue of slavery to the larger goal of securing the unity and independence of the United States.

Nevertheless, the Founders, with the exception of those from South Carolina and Georgia, exhibited considerable aversion to slavery during the era of the Articles of Confederation (1781–89) by prohibiting the importation of foreign slaves to individual states and lending their support to a proposal by Jefferson to ban slavery in the Northwest Territory. Such antislavery policies, however, only went so far. The prohibition of foreign slave imports, by limiting the foreign supply, conveniently served the interests of Virginia and Maryland slaveholders, who could then sell their own surplus slaves southward and westward at higher prices. Furthermore, the ban on slavery in the Northwest tacitly legitimated the expansion of slavery in the Southwest.

Despite initial disagreements over slavery at the Constitutional Convention in 1787, the Founders once again demonstrated their commitment to maintaining the unity of the new United States by resolving to diffuse sectional tensions over slavery. To this end the Founders drafted a series of constitutional clauses acknowledging deep-seated regional differences over slavery while requiring all sections of the new country to make compromises as well. They granted slaveholding states the right to count three-fifths of their slave population when it came to apportioning the number of a state's representatives to Congress, thereby enhancing Southern power in the House of Representatives. But they also used this same ratio to determine the federal tax contribution required of each state, thus increasing the direct federal tax burden of slaveholding states. Georgians and South Carolinians won a moratorium until 1808 on any congressional ban against the importation of slaves, but in the meantime individual states remained free to prohibit slave imports if they so wished. Southerners also obtained the inclusion of a fugitive slave clause) designed to encourage the return of runaway slaves who sought refuge in free states, but the Constitution left enforcement of this clause to the cooperation of the states rather than to the coercion of Congress.

Although the Founders, consistent with their beliefs in limited government, opposed granting the new federal government significant authority over slavery, several individual Northern Founders promoted antislavery causes at the state level. Benjamin Franklin in Pennsylvania, as well as John Jay and Alexander Hamilton in New York, served as officers in their respective state antislavery societies. The prestige they lent to these organizations ultimately contributed to the gradual abolition of slavery in each of the Northern states.

Although slavery was legal in every Northern state at the beginning of the American Revolution, its economic impact was marginal. As a result, Northern Founders were freer to explore the libertarian dimensions of Revolutionary ideology. The experience of Franklin was in many ways typical of the evolving attitudes of Northern Founders toward slavery. Although enmeshed in the slave system for much of his life, Franklin eventually came to believe that slavery ought to be abolished gradually and legally. Franklin himself had owned slaves, run ads in his Pennsylvania Gazette to secure the return of fugitive slaves, and defended the honour of slaveholding revolutionaries. By 1781, however, Franklin had divested himself of slaves, and shortly thereafter he became the president of the Pennsylvania Abolition Society. He also went further than most of his contemporaries by signing a petition to the First Federal Congress in 1790 for the abolition of slavery and the slave trade.

Unlike their Northern counterparts, Southern Founders generally steered clear of organized antislavery activities, primarily to maintain their legitimacy among slaveholding constituents. Furthermore, while a few Northern and Southern Founders manumitted a small number of slaves, no Southern plantation-owning Founder, except George Washington, freed a sizeable body of enslaved labourers. Because his own slaves shared familial attachments with the dower slaves of his wife, Martha Custis Washington, he sought to convince her heirs to forego their inheritance rights in favour of a collective manumission so as to ensure that entire families, not just individual family members, might be freed. Washington failed to win the consent of the Custis heirs, but he nevertheless made sure, through his last will and testament, that his own slaves would enjoy the benefit of freedom.

Washington's act of manumission implied that he could envision a biracial United States where both blacks and whites might live together as free people. Jefferson, however, explicitly rejected this vision. He acknowledged that slavery violated the natural rights of slaves and that conflicts over slavery might one day lead to the dissolution of the union, but he also believed that, given alleged innate racial differences and deeply held prejudices, emancipation would inevitably degrade the character of the republic and unleash violent civil strife between blacks and whites. Jefferson thus advocated coupling emancipation with what he called "colonization," or removal, of the black population beyond the boundaries of the United States. His proposals won considerable support in the North, where racial prejudice was on the rise, but such schemes found little support among the majority of Southern slaveholders.

When the last remaining Founders died in the 1830s, they left behind an ambiguous legacy with regard to slavery. They had succeeded in gradually abolishing slavery in the Northern states and Northwestern territories but permitted its rapid expansion in the South and Southwest. Although they eventually enacted a federal ban on the importation of foreign slaves in 1808, the enslaved population continued to expand through natural reproduction, while the growing internal domestic slave trade led to an increase in the tragic breakup of enslaved families.

But the Congress was endowed with the basic powers of a modern—and sovereign—government. This was a republic, and the United States could confer no aristocratic titles of honour. The prospect of eventual enlargement of federal power appeared in the clause giving the Congress powers to pass legislation "necessary and proper" for implementing the general purposes of the Constitution.

The states retained their civil jurisdiction, but there was an emphatic

Cartoon depicting attacks on the Pennsylvania state constitution by self-interest groups. Library of Congress, Washington, D.C.

shift of the political centre of gravity to the federal government, of which the most fundamental indication was the universal understanding that this government would act directly on citizens, as individuals, throughout all the states, regardless of state authority. The language of the Constitution told of the new style: it began, "We the people of the United States," rather than "We the people of New Hampshire, Massachusetts, etc."

THE RESPONSE TO FEDERALISM

The draft Constitution aroused widespread opposition. Anti-Federalists—

so-called because their opponents deftly seized the appellation of "Federalists," though they were really nationalists—were strong in states such as Virginia, New York, and Massachusetts, where the economy was relatively success-ful and many people saw little need for such extreme remedies. Anti-Federalists also expressed fears—here touches of class conflict certainly arose—that the new government would fall into the hands of merchants and men of money. Many good republicans detected oligar-chy in the structure of the Senate, with its six-year terms. The absence of a bill of rights aroused deep fears of central power. The Federalists, however, had the advantages of communications, the press, organization, and, generally, the better of the argument. Anti-Federalists also suffered the disadvantage of hav-ing no internal coherence or unified purpose.

The debate gave rise to an inten-sive literature, much of it at a very high level. The most sustained pro-Federalist argument, written mainly by Hamilton and Madison (assisted by Jay) under the pseudonym Publius, appeared in the newspapers as *The Federalist*. These essays attacked the feebleness of the confederation and claimed that the new Constitution would have advantages for all sectors of society while threaten-ing none. In the course of the debate, they passed from a strongly national-ist standpoint to one that showed more respect for the idea of a mixed form of

Alexander Hamilton, detail of an oil painting by John Trumbull; in the National Gallery of Art, Washington, D.C. Courtesy of the National Gallery of Art, Washington, D.C., Andrew Mellon Collection

government that would safeguard the states. Madison contributed assurances that a multiplicity of interests would counteract each other, preventing the consolidation of power continually charged by their enemies.

The Bill of Rights, steered through the first Congress by Madison's diplomacy, mollified much of the latent opposition. These first 10 amendments, ratified in 1791, adopted into the Constitution the basic English common-law rights that

Document: The Federalist Papers (1787–88)

Between October 1787 and August 1788, Alexander Hamilton, John Jay, and James Madison wrote a series of essays that appeared in various New York newspapers under the pseudonym "Publius." The Federalist, as the combined essays are called, was written to combat anti-federalism. Hoping to persuade the public of the necessity for the Constitution, Publius gave excellent arguments for adopting it and discarding the Articles. The Federalist stresses the urgent need for an adequate central government and the ease with which the republican form of government would be adapted to the large expanse of territory and widely divergent interests found in the United States. It was immediately recognized as the most powerful defense of the new Constitution and hailed as a classic in constitutional theory. Jefferson called The Federalist "the best commentary on the principles of government which ever was written." Of the 85 essays, John Jay definitely wrote 5, Madison 26, and Hamilton 51. The authorship of the other three is in doubt. Included here are excerpts from Federalist papers No. 1 by Hamilton and No. 14 by Madison, beginning with the former.

After an unequivocal experience of the inefficiency of the subsisting federal government, you are called upon to deliberate on a new Constitution for the United States of America. The subject speaks its own importance; comprehending in its consequences nothing less than the existence of the Union, the safety and welfare of the parts of which it is composed, the fate of an empire in many respects the most interesting in the world. It has been frequently remarked that it seems to have been reserved to the people of this country, by their conduct and example, to decide the important question, whether societies of men are really capable or not of establishing good government from reflection and choice, or whether they are forever destined to depend for their political constitutions on accident and force. If there be any truth in the remark, the crisis at which we are arrived may with propriety be regarded as the era in which that decision is to be made; and a wrong election of the part we shall act may, in this view, deserve to be considered as the general misfortune of mankind.

This idea will add the inducements of philanthropy to those of patriotism, to heighten the solicitude which all considerate and good men must feel for the event. Happy will it be if our choice should be directed by a judicious estimate of our true interests, unperplexed and unbiased by considerations not connected with the public good. But this is a thing more ardently to be wished than seriously to be expected. The plan offered to our deliberations affects too many particular interests, innovates upon too many local institutions, not to involve in its discussion a variety of objects foreign to its merits, and of views, passions, and prejudices little favorable to the discovery of truth....

Americans had fought for. But they did more. Unlike Britain, the United States secured a guarantee of freedom for the press and the right of (peaceable) assembly. Also unlike Britain, church and state were formally separated in a clause that seemed to set equal value on nonestablishment of religion and its free

Document: The Bill of Rights (1789)

In the three and a half months during which the proposed amendments to the Constitution were before Congress, only seven or eight days were actually spent in debating them. On Sept. 25, 1789, final drafts of 12 amendments (out of the many that had been suggested by James Madison and others) were passed by Congress and presented to the states for approval. Two of the 12 were never ratified; they would have limited the number of members of the House of Representatives and prevented the members of Congress from raising their salaries without an election intervening. On Dec. 15, 1791, when Virginia became the 11th state to ratify them, the other 10 proposed amendments or additions to the Constitution, which are reprinted here, became part of the supreme law of the land. The so-called Bill of Rights, as finally ratified, was generally modeled after the Virginia Declaration of Rights of 1776. Its significant contribution was to put into writing as part of a constitution those protections against government encroachment that had often been assumed, but not before so explicitly defined.

ARTICLE I
Congress shall make no law respecting an establishment of religion or prohibiting the free exercise thereof, or abridging the freedom of speech or of the press, or the right of the people peaceably to assemble and to petition the government for a redress of grievances.

ARTICLE II
A well-regulated militia being necessary to the security of a free state, the right of the people to keep and bear arms shall not be infringed.

ARTICLE III
No soldier shall, in time of peace, be quartered in any house without the consent of the owner, nor in time of war but in a manner to be prescribed by law.

ARTICLE IV
The right of the people to be secure in their persons, houses, papers, and effects against unreasonable searches and seizures shall not be violated, and no warrants shall issue, but upon probable cause, supported by oath or affirmation, and particularly describing the place to be searched and the persons or things to be seized.

ARTICLE V
No person shall be held to answer for a capital or otherwise infamous crime unless on a presentment or indictment of a grand jury, except in cases arising in the land or naval forces, or in the militia, when in actual service in time of war or public danger; nor shall any person be subject for the same offense to be twice put in jeopardy of life or limb; nor shall be compelled in any criminal case to be a witness against himself, nor be deprived of life, liberty, or property without due process of law; nor shall private property be taken for public use without just compensation....

The Bill of Rights. National Archives, Washington, D.C.

exercise. (This left the states free to maintain their own establishments.)

In state conventions held through the winter of 1787 to the summer of 1788, the Constitution was ratified by the necessary minimum of nine states. But the vote was desperately close in Virginia and New York, respectively the 10th and 11th states to ratify, and without them the whole scheme would have been built on sand.

CHAPTER 6

THE SOCIAL REVOLUTION

The American Revolution was a great social upheaval but one that was widely diffused, often gradual, and different in different regions. Change came, but not for everyone and not in equal measure. Class divides persisted, and political and economic power remained largely restricted to the privileged few. Still, change was real, and life improved demonstrably for many. Perhaps more important, even more sweeping changes began to seem possible.

SLAVERY

The principles of liberty and equality stood in stark conflict with the institution of African slavery, which had built much of the country's wealth. One gradual effect of this conflict was the decline of slavery in all the Northern states; another was a spate of manumissions by liberal slave owners in Virginia. But with most slave owners, especially in South Carolina and Georgia, ideals counted for nothing. Throughout the slave states, the institution of slavery came to be reinforced by a white supremacist doctrine of racial inferiority. The manumissions did result in the development

Sale of Estates, Pictures, and Slaves in the Rotunda, New Orleans, 1842. Library of Congress, Washington, D.C.

of new communities of free blacks, who enjoyed considerable freedom of movement for a few years and who produced some outstanding figures, such as the astronomer Benjamin Banneker and the religious leader Richard Allen, a founder of the African Methodist Episcopal Church Zion. But in the 1790s and after, the condition of free blacks deteriorated as states adopted laws restricting their activities, residences, and economic choices. In general they came to occupy poor neighbourhoods and grew into a permanent underclass, denied education and opportunity.

THE ROLE OF WOMEN

The American Revolution also dramatized the economic importance of women. Women had always contributed indispensably to the operation of farms and often businesses, while they seldom acquired independent status. However, when war removed men from the locality, women often had to

Document: Petition by Free African Americans for Equality Under the Law (1791)

Throughout the country's first century, African Americans, slave or free, were severely restricted by laws in both the North and the South. Many states had laws prohibiting them from bringing a suit against another party or even testifying under oath in a court. One of the earliest protests against these laws is excerpted below. It was presented in January 1791, to the South Carolina legislature by a group of African Americans in Charleston.

To the Honorable David Ramsay, Esquire, president, and to the rest of the honorable new members of the Senate of the state of South Carolina,

The memorial of Thomas Cole, bricklayer, P. B. Mathews and Mathew Webb, butchers, on behalf of themselves and others, free men of color, humbly shows:

That in the enumeration of free citizens by the Constitution of the United States for the purpose of representation of the Southern states in Congress your memorialists have been considered under that description as part of the citizens of this state.

Although by the fourteenth and twenty-ninth clauses in an Act of Assembly made in the year 1740 and entitled an Act for the Better Ordering and Governing Negroes and Other Slaves in this Province, commonly called the Negro Act, now in force, your memorialists are deprived of the rights and privileges of citizens by not having it in their power to give testimony on oath in prosecutions on behalf of the state; from which cause many culprits have escaped the punishment due to their atrocious crimes, nor can they give their testimony in recovering debts due to them, or in establishing agreements made by them within the meaning of the Statutes of Frauds and Perjuries in force in this state except in cases where persons of color are concerned, whereby they are subject to great losses and repeated injuries without any means of redress.

That by the said clauses in the said Act, they are debarred of the rights of free citizens by being subject to a trial without the benefit of a jury and subject to prosecution by testimony of slaves without oath by which they are placed on the same footing....

take full charge, which they proved they could do. Republican ideas spread among women, influencing discussion of women's rights, education, and role in society. Some states modified their inheritance and property laws to permit women to inherit a share of estates and to exercise limited control of property after marriage. On the whole, however, the Revolution itself had only very gradual and diffused effects on women's ultimate status. Such changes as took place amounted to a fuller recognition of the importance of women as mothers of republican citizens rather than making them into independent citizens of equal political and civil status with men.

Document: Abigail Adams: Doubts About Independence (1775)

Although Abigail Adams had little formal education, she was intelligent and broad-minded and became a terse and vigorous letter writer.

That she was concerned with the growth of the new country can be seen in her numerous letters to her husband, John Adams. In the following letter, written Nov. 27, 1775, she expresses her doubts about the ability of the Americans to form a viable government.

Colonel Warren returned last week to Plymouth, so that I shall not hear anything from you until he goes back again, which will not be till the last of this month. He damped my spirits greatly by telling me that the court had prolonged your stay another month. I was pleasing myself with the thought that you would soon be upon your return. It is in vain to repine. I hope the public will reap what I sacrifice.

I wish I knew what mighty things were fabricating. If a form of government is to be established here, what one will be assumed? Will it be left to our assemblies to choose one? And will not many men have many minds? And shall we not run into dissensions among ourselves? I am more and more convinced that man is a dangerous creature; and that power, whether vested in many or a few, is ever grasping, and, like the grave, cries "Give, give." The great fish swallow up the small; and he who is most strenuous for the rights of the people when vested with power, is as eager after the prerogatives of government. You tell me of degrees of perfection to which human nature is capable of arriving, and I believe it, but, at the same time, lament that our admiration should arise from the scarcity of the instances....

Abigail Adams, oil painting by Gilbert Stuart. Library of Congress Prints and Photographs Division

LEGAL REFORM

Americans had fought for independence to protect common-law rights; they had no program for legal reform. Gradually, however, some customary practices came to seem out of keeping with republican principles. The outstanding example was the law of inheritance. The new states took steps, where necessary, to remove the old rule of primogeniture in favour of equal partition of intestate estates. This conformed to both the egalitarian and the individualist principles preferred by American society. Humanization of the penal codes, however, occurred only gradually, in the 19th century, inspired as much by European example as by American sentiment.

RELIGIOUS REVIVALISM

Religion played a central role in the emergence of a distinctively "American" society in the first years of independence. Several key developments took place. One was the creation of American denominations independent of their British and European origins and leadership. By 1789 American Anglicans (renaming themselves Episcopalians), Methodists (formerly Wesleyans), Roman Catholics, and members of various Baptist, Lutheran, and Dutch Reformed congregations had established organizations and chosen leaders who were born in or full-time residents of what had become the United States of America. Another pivotal postindependence development was a rekindling of religious enthusiasm, especially on the frontier, that opened the gates of religious activism to the laity. Still another was the disestablishment of tax-supported churches in those states most deeply feeling the impact of democratic diversity. And finally, this period saw the birth of a liberal and socially aware version of Christianity uniting Enlightenment values with American activism.

Between 1798 and 1800 a sudden burst of revitalization shook frontier Protestant congregations, beginning with a great revival in Logan county, Ky., under the leadership of men such as James McGready and the brothers John and William McGee. This was followed by a gigantic camp meeting at Cane Ridge, where thousands were "converted." The essence of the frontier revival was that this conversion from mere formal Christianity to a full conviction in God's mercy for the sinner was a deeply emotional experience accessible even to those with much faith and little learning. So exhorters who were barely literate themselves could preach brimstone and fire and showers of grace, bringing repentant listeners to a state of excitement in which they would weep and groan, writhe and faint, and undergo physical transports in full public view.

"Heart religion" supplanted "head religion." For the largely Scotch-Irish Presbyterian ministers in the West, this led to dangerous territory, because the official church leadership preferred more decorum and biblical scholarship from its pastors. Moreover, the idea of winning salvation by noisy penitence undercut Calvinist predestination. In fact, the fracture along fault lines of class and geography led to several schisms. Methodism had fewer problems of this kind. It never embraced predestination, and, more to the point, its structure was democratic, with rudimentarily educated lay preachers able to rise from leading individual congregations to presiding over districts and regional "conferences,"

Document: A Plan of Union for Protestant Churches (1801)

Though the era of the Great Awakening, which first arose in the 1730s and experienced a renewal in the 1790s, was marked by a revived interest in religious questions, it also gave rise to varying interpretations of the Bible and thus to a proliferation of small sects throughout the country. But the resulting diffusion of popular support made it almost inevitable that some efforts should be made to combine resources and endeavours. In 1801 the Congregational Association of Connecticut and the General Assembly of the Presbyterian Church joined forces for the stated purpose of multiplying churches and winning the unconverted throughout the northern states and territories. The so-called Plan of Union provided that Congregational ministers could serve in Presbyterian congregations and vice versa. Cooperation between these two churches was possible in part because of their common Calvinistic heritage. The Plan, which is reprinted below, was relatively short-lived, but it was a significant step toward understanding among the Protestant denominations.

- It is strictly enjoined on all their missionaries to the new settlements to endeavor by all proper means to promote mutual forbearance and a spirit of accommodation between those inhabitants of the new settlements who hold the Presbyterian and those who hold the Congregational form of church government.
- If, in the new settlements, any church of the Congregational order shall settle a minister of the Presbyterian order, that church may, if they choose, still conduct their discipline according to Congregational principles, settling their difficulties among themselves or by a council mutually agreed upon for that purpose. But if any difficulty shall exist between the minister and the church or any member of it, it shall be referred to the presbytery to which the minister shall belong, provided both parties agree to it; if not, to a council consisting of an equal number of Presbyterians and Congregationalists, agreed upon by both parties.
- If a Presbyterian church shall settle a minister of Congregational principles, that church may still conduct their discipline according to Presbyterian principles, excepting that if a difficulty arise between him and his church, or any member of it, the cause shall be tried by the association to which the said minister shall belong, provided both parties agree to it, otherwise by a council, one-half Congregationalists and the other half Presbyterians, mutually agreed upon by the parties....

eventually embracing the entire church membership. Methodism fitted very neatly into frontier conditions through its use of traveling ministers, or circuit riders, who rode from isolated settlement to settlement, saving souls and mightily liberalizing the word of God.

The revival spirit rolled back eastward to inspire a "Second Great Awakening," especially in New England, that emphasized gatherings that were less uninhibited than camp meetings but warmer than conventional Congregational and Presbyterian services. Ordained

Early 19th-century Methodist camp meeting. Library of Congress, Washington, D.C.

and college-educated ministers such as Lyman Beecher made it their mission to promote revivalism as a counterweight to the Deism of some of the Founding Fathers and the atheism of the French Revolution. Revivals also gave churches a new grasp on the loyalties of their congregations through lay participation in spreading the good word of salvation. This voluntarism more than offset the gradual state-by-state cancellation of taxpayer support for individual denominations.

The era of the early republic also saw the growth, especially among the urban educated elite of Boston, of a gentler form of Christianity embodied in Unitarianism, which rested on the notion of an essentially benevolent God who made his will known to humankind through their exercise of the reasoning powers bestowed on them. In the Unitarian view, Jesus Christ was simply a great moral teacher. Many Christians of the "middling" sort viewed Unitarianism as excessively concerned with ideas and social reform and far too indulgent or indifferent to the existence of sin and Satan. By 1815, then, the social structure of American Protestantism, firmly embedded in many activist forms in the national culture, had taken shape.

CHAPTER 7

FROM 1789 TO 1816

The first elections under the new Constitution were held in 1789. George Washington was unanimously voted the country's first president. Washington's administration of the government in the next eight years was marked by the caution, methodical precision, and sober judgment that had always characterized him. He regarded himself as standing aloof from party divisions and emphasized his position as president of the whole country by touring first through the Northern states and later through the Southern.

THE FEDERALIST ADMINISTRATION AND THE FORMATION OF PARTIES

In selecting the four members of his first cabinet—Thomas Jefferson as secretary of state, Alexander Hamilton as secretary of treasury, Henry Knox as secretary of war, and Edmund Randolph as attorney general—Washington balanced the two parties evenly. Alexander Hamilton formed a clear-cut program that soon gave substance to the old fears of the Anti-Federalists. Hamilton, who had believed since the early 1780s that a national debt would be "a national blessing," both for economic reasons and because it would act as a "cement"

Triumphal arches, such as these near Philadelphia, were erected throughout the United States to commemorate the inauguration of Pres. George Washington on April 30, 1789. Library of Congress, Washington, D.C.

to the union, used his new power base to realize the ambitions of the nationalists. He recommended that the federal government pay off the old Continental Congress's debts at par rather than at a depreciated value and that it assume state debts, drawing the interests of the creditors toward the central government rather than state governments. This plan met strong opposition from the many who had sold their securities at great discount during the postwar depression and from Southern states, which had repudiated their debts and did not want to be taxed to pay other states' debts. A compromise in Congress was reached—thanks to the efforts of Secretary of State Jefferson—whereby Southern states approved Hamilton's plan in return for

Northern agreement to fix the location of the new national capital on the banks of the Potomac, closer to the South. When Hamilton next introduced his plan to found a Bank of the United States, modeled on the Bank of England, opposition began to harden. Many argued that the Constitution did not confide this power to Congress. Hamilton, however, persuaded Washington that anything not expressly forbidden by the Constitution was permitted under implied powers—the beginning of "loose" as opposed to "strict" constructionist interpretations of the Constitution. The Bank Act passed in 1791. Hamilton also advocated plans for the support of nascent industry, which proved premature, and he imposed the revenue-raising whiskey excise that led to the Whiskey Rebellion, a minor uprising in western Pennsylvania in 1794.

A party opposed to Hamilton's fiscal policies began to form in Congress. With Madison at its centre and with support from Jefferson, it soon extended its appeal beyond Congress to popular constituencies. Meanwhile, the French Revolution and France's subsequent declaration of war against Great Britain, Spain, and Holland further divided American loyalties. Democratic-Republican societies sprang up to express support for France, while

Hamilton and his supporters, known as Federalists, backed Britain for economic reasons. Washington pronounced American neutrality in Europe, but to prevent a war with Britain he sent Chief Justice John Jay to London to negotiate a treaty. In the Jay Treaty (1794) the United States gained only minor concessions and—humiliatingly—accepted British naval supremacy as the price of protection for American shipping.

Washington, whose tolerance had been severely strained by the Whiskey Rebellion and by criticism of the Jay

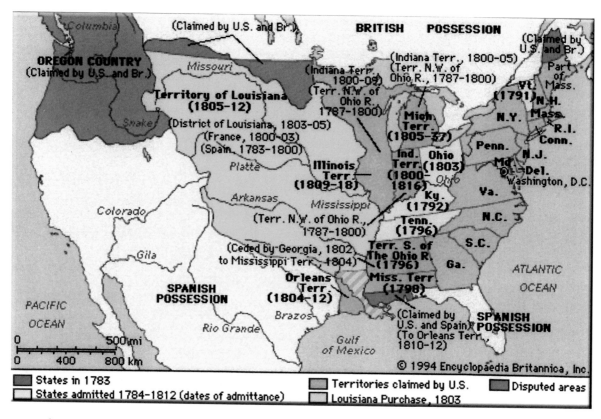

The United States, 1783–1812.

Document: George Washington: Farewell Address (1796)

George Washington's Farewell Address was never delivered by him. It appeared first by his own arrangement in a newspaper at Philadelphia, then the seat of the national government. Designed in part to remove him from consideration for a third term as president of the United States, the address as published was similar to one he had prepared at the end of his first term, in 1792, when he had contemplated retiring from office. In July 1796, he sent a copy of this earlier address to Alexander Hamilton, requesting him to write a new one. Hamilton, who until the year before had been secretary of the treasury and the chief architect of Washington's administration, did as he was asked, but the result, again reworked by Washington, still reflects the ideas of the retiring president. It was printed in the American Daily Advertiser, *Sept. 19, 1796.*

Friends and Fellow Citizens:

The period for a new election of a citizen to administer the executive government of the United States being not far distant, and the time actually arrived when your thoughts must be employed in designating the person who is to be clothed with that important trust, it appears to me proper, especially as it may conduce to a more distinct expression of the public voice, that I should now apprise you of the resolution I have formed to decline being considered among the number of those out of whom a choice is to be made. I beg you, at the same time, to do me the justice to be assured that this resolution has not been taken without a strict regard to all the considerations appertaining to the relation which binds a dutiful citizen to his country; and that, in withdrawing the tender of service which silence in my situation might imply, I am influenced by no diminution of zeal for your future interest, no deficiency of grateful respect for your past kindness, but act under ... a full conviction that the step is compatible with both. The acceptance of and continuance hitherto in the office to which your suffrages have twice called me have been a uniform sacrifice of inclination to the opinion of duty and to a deference for what appeared to be your desire. I constantly hoped that it would have been much earlier in my power, consistently with motives which I was not at liberty to disregard, to return to that retirement from which I had been reluctantly drawn. The strength of my inclination to do this, previous to the last election, had even led to the preparation of an address to declare it to you; but mature reflection on the then perplexed and critical posture of our affairs with foreign nations, and the unanimous advice of persons entitled to my confidence, impelled me to abandon the idea....

Treaty, chose not to run for a third presidential term. In his Farewell Address, in a passage drafted by Hamilton, he denounced the new party politics as divisive and dangerous.

Parties did not yet aspire to national objectives, however, and, when the Federalist John Adams was elected president, the Democrat-Republican Jefferson, as the presidential candidate

John Adams, oil painting by Gilbert Stuart, 1826. Smithsonian American Art Museum, Washington, D.C./Art Resource, New York

Later that year the Federalist majority in Congress passed the Alien and Sedition Acts, which imposed serious civil restrictions on aliens suspected of pro-French activities and penalized U.S. citizens who criticized the government, making nonsense of the First Amendment's guarantee of free press. The acts were most often invoked to prosecute Republican editors, some of whom served jail terms. These measures in turn called forth the Virginia and Kentucky resolutions, drafted respectively by Madison and Jefferson, which invoked state sovereignty against intolerable federal powers. War with France often seemed imminent during this period, but Adams was determined to avoid issuing a formal declaration of war, and in this he succeeded.

Taxation, which had been levied to pay anticipated war costs, brought more discontent, however, including a new minor rising in Pennsylvania led by Jacob Fries. Fries's Rebellion was put down without difficulty, but widespread disagreement over issues ranging from civil liberties to taxation was polarizing American politics. A basic sense of political identity now divided Federalists from Republicans, and in the election of 1800 Jefferson drew on deep sources of Anti-Federalist opposition to challenge

with the second greatest number of votes, became vice president. Wars in Europe and on the high seas, together with rampant opposition at home, gave the new administration little peace. Virtual naval war with France had followed from American acceptance of British naval protection. In 1798 a French attempt to solicit bribes from American commissioners negotiating a settlement of differences (the so-called XYZ Affair) aroused a wave of anti-French feeling.

and defeat his old friend and colleague Adams. The result was the first contest over the presidency between political parties and the first actual change of government as a result of a general election in modern history.

THE JEFFERSONIAN REPUBLICANS IN POWER

Jefferson began his presidency with a plea for reconciliation: "We are all Republicans, we are all Federalists." He had no plans for a permanent two-party system of government. He also began with a strong commitment to limited government and strict construction of the Constitution. All these commitments were soon to be tested by the exigencies of war, diplomacy, and political contingency.

On the American continent, Jefferson pursued a policy of expansion. He seized the opportunity when Napoleon I decided to relinquish French ambitions in North America by offering the Louisiana territory for sale (Spain had recently ceded the territory to France). This extraordinary acquisition, the Louisiana Purchase, bought at a price of a few cents per acre, more than doubled the area of the United States. Jefferson had no constitutional

The 1803 Louisiana Purchase more than doubled the area of the United States for $15 million.

Document: Thomas Jefferson: The Politics of the Louisiana Purchase (1803)

When Napoleon was induced to sell the Louisiana Territory to the United States on April 30, 1803, many questions were raised by the purchase. The Constitution made no provision for a transaction of this nature, and many wondered whether the federal government had the right to increase the national domain through a negotiated sale with a foreign country. If such power existed, did the government have the further right to promise statehood to persons living outside the original states? In a letter of Aug. 12, 1803, Pres. Thomas Jefferson discussed these matters with John Breckinridge, his friend and political lieutenant, who had introduced his Kentucky Resolutions into the Kentucky legislature in 1798. Realizing that protests, especially from the Federalist camp, could block the congressional acceptance of the treaty, Jefferson beseeched Breckinridge, in a letter of August 18, not to divulge their correspondence. As a final preventive measure, in case the purchase was blocked on constitutional grounds, an amendment was prepared to incorporate the territory directly into the Union. The two Jefferson letters and the amendment are reprinted here, beginning with the letter of August 18.

The enclosed letter...gives me occasion to write a word to you on the subject of Louisiana, which, being a new one, an interchange of sentiments may produce correct ideas before we are to act on them.

Our information as to the country is very incomplete. We have taken measures to obtain it in full as to the settled part, which I hope to receive in time for Congress. The boundaries, which I deem not admitting question, are the highlands on the western side of the Mississippi enclosing all its waters, the Missouri, of course, and terminating in the line drawn from the northwestern point of the Lake of the Woods to the nearest source of the Mississippi, as lately settled between Great Britain and the United States. We have some claims to extend on the seacoast westwardly to the Rio Norte or Bravo [Rio Grande], and, better, to go eastwardly to the Rio Perdido, between Mobile and Pensacola, the ancient boundary of Louisiana. These claims will be a subject of negotiation with Spain and if, as soon as she is at war, we push them strongly with one hand, holding out a price in the other, we shall certainly obtain the Floridas, and all in good time.

In the meanwhile, without waiting for permission, we shall enter into the exercise of the natural right we have always insisted on with Spain, to wit, that of a nation holding the upper part of streams having a right of innocent passage through them to the ocean. We shall prepare her to see us practise on this, and she will not oppose it by force....

sanction for such an exercise of executive power. He made up the rules as he went along, taking a broad construction view of the Constitution on this issue. He also sought opportunities to gain Florida from Spain, and, for scientific and political reasons, he sent Meriwether Lewis and William Clark on an expedition of exploration across the continent. This territorial expansion was not without problems. Various separatist movements periodically arose, including a plan for a Northern Confederacy formulated by New England Federalists. Aaron Burr, who had been elected Jefferson's vice president in 1800 but was replaced in 1804, led several western conspiracies. Arrested and tried for treason, he was acquitted in 1807.

As chief executive, Jefferson clashed with members of the judiciary, many of whom had been late appointments by Adams. One of his primary opponents was the late appointee Chief Justice John Marshall, most notably in the case of *Marbury* v. *Madison* (1803), in which the Supreme Court first exercised the power of judicial review of congressional legislation.

By the start of Jefferson's second term in office, Europe was engulfed in the Napoleonic Wars. The United States remained neutral, but both Britain and France imposed various orders and decrees severely restricting American trade with Europe and confiscated American ships for violating the new rules. Britain also conducted impressment raids in which U.S. citizens were sometimes seized. Unable to agree to treaty terms with Britain, Jefferson tried to coerce both Britain and France into ceasing to violate "neutral rights" with a total embargo on American exports, enacted by Congress in 1807. The results were catastrophic for American commerce and produced bitter alienation in

John Marshall, crayon portrait by Charles-Balthazar-Julien Févret de Saint-Mémin; in the Duke University Law School, Durham, North Carolina. Courtesy of Duke University, Durham, N.C.

New England, where the embargo (written backward as "O grab me") was held to be a Southern plot to destroy New England's wealth. In 1809, shortly after Madison was elected president, the embargo act was repealed.

MADISON AS PRESIDENT AND THE WAR OF 1812

Madison's presidency was dominated by foreign affairs. Both Britain and France committed depredations on American shipping, but Britain was more resented, partly because with the greatest navy it

Cartoon from 1812 showing Columbia (the United States) warning Napoleon I that she will deal with him after teaching John Bull (England) a lesson. Library of Congress, Washington, D.C.

was more effective and partly because Americans were extremely sensitive to British insults to national honour. Certain expansionist elements looking to both Florida and Canada began to press for war and took advantage of the issue of naval protection. Madison's own aim was to preserve the principle of freedom of the seas and to assert the ability of the United States to protect its own interests and its citizens. While striving to confront the European adversaries impartially, he was drawn into war against Britain, which was declared in June 1812 on a vote of 79–49 in the House and 19–13

in the Senate. There was almost no support for war in the strong Federalist New England states.

The War of 1812 began and ended in irony. The British had already rescinded the offending orders in council, but the news had not reached the United States at the time of the declaration. The Americans were poorly placed from every point of view. Ideological objections to armies and navies had been responsible for a minimal naval force. Ideological objections to banks had been responsible, in 1812, for the Senate's refusal to renew

A tableau of the Treaty of Ghent, signed in Belgium, Dec. 24, 1814. Library of Congress, Washington, D.C.

the charter of the Bank of the United States. Mercantile sentiment was hostile to the administration. Under the circumstances, it was remarkable that the United States succeeded in staggering through two years of war, eventually winning important naval successes at sea, on the Great Lakes, and on Lake Champlain. On land a British raiding party burned public buildings in Washington, D.C., and drove President Madison to flee from the capital. The only action with long-term implications was Andrew Jackson's victory at the Battle of New Orleans—won in January 1815, two weeks after peace had been achieved with the signing of the Treaty of Ghent (Belgium). Jackson's political reputation rose directly from this battle.

In historical retrospect, the most important aspect of the peace settlement was an agreement to set up a boundary commission for the Canadian border, which could thenceforth be left unguarded. It was not the end of Anglo-American hostility, but the agreement marked the advent of an era of mutual trust. The conclusion of the War of 1812, which has sometimes been called the Second War of American Independence, marked a historical cycle. It resulted in a pacification of the old feelings of pain and resentment against Great Britain and its people—still for many Americans a kind of paternal relationship. And, by freeing them of anxieties on this front, it also freed Americans to look to the West.

THE INDIAN-AMERICAN PROBLEM

The young United States believed that it had inherited an "Indian problem," but it would be equally fair to say that the victory at Yorktown confronted the Indians with an insoluble "American

Document: Red Jacket: Against White Missions Among the Indians (1805)

The missionary impulse to Christianize the Native Americans that marked the early Puritan settlers in America was also a major characteristic of the 18th-century religious revival known as the Great Awakening. Missionary societies, which continued to function into the 19th century, worked at the conversion of Native Americans with a single-minded zeal that could only be produced by the certainty of the eternal damnation that would otherwise be their lot. In the summer of 1805, a number of the principal chiefs and warriors of the Six Nations, principally Senecas, assembled at Buffalo Creek in the state of New York at the request of a certain Reverend Cram from the Boston Missionary Society. The following eloquent speech of the Seneca Chief, Red Jacket, was prompted by the somewhat tactless remarks and questions put to the chiefs and warriors by Cram. Red Jacket, whose Indian name was Sagoyewatha, had little sympathy with the way in which the white man's customs were being foisted on his people.

Friend and brother, it was the will of the Great Spirit that we should meet together this day. He orders all things and has given us a fine day for our council. He has taken His garment from before the sun and caused it to shine with brightness upon us. Our eyes are opened, that we see clearly; our ears are unstopped, that we have been able to hear distinctly the words you have spoken. For all these favors we thank the Great Spirit, and Him only.

Brother, this council fire was kindled by you. It was at your request that we came together at this time. We have listened with attention to what you have said. You requested us to speak our minds freely. This gives us great joy, for we now consider that we stand upright before you and can speak what we think. All have heard your voice, and all speak to you now as one man. Our minds are agreed.

Brother, you say you want an answer to your talk before you leave this place. It is right you should have one as you are a great distance from home and we do not wish to detain you. But we will first look back a little and tell you what our fathers have told us and what we have heard from the white people.

Brother, listen to what we say....

An American cartoon attacking the alliance between the "Humane British" and the Indians during the War of 1812. Library of Congress, Washington, D.C.

problem." Whereas they had earlier dealt with representatives of Europe-based empires seeking only access to selected resources from a distant continent, now they faced a resident, united people yearly swelling in numbers, determined to make every acre of the West their own and culturally convinced of their absolute title under the laws of God and history. There was no room for compromise. Even before 1776, each step toward American independence reduced the Indians' control over their own future. The Proclamation Line of 1763 was almost immediately violated by men like Daniel Boone on the Kentucky frontier. In the western parts of Pennsylvania and New York, however, despite extensive Indian land concessions in the 1768 Treaty of Fort Stanwix, they still had enough power to bar an advance toward the Ohio Valley and the Great Lakes.

For armed resistance to have had any hope of success, unity would be required between all the Indians from the Appalachians to the Mississippi. This unity simply could not be achieved. The Shawnee leaders known as Tenskatawa, or the Prophet, and his brother Tecumseh attempted this kind of rallying movement, much as Pontiac had done some 40 years earlier, with equal lack of success. Some help was forthcoming in the form of arms from British traders remaining in the Northwest Territory in violation of the peace treaty, but the Indians failed to secure victory in a clash with American militia and regulars at the Battle of Tippecanoe Creek (near present-day West Lafayette, Ind.) in 1811.

The outbreak of the War of 1812 sparked renewed Indian hopes of protection by the crown, should the British win. Tecumseh himself was actually commissioned as a general in the royal forces; but, at the Battle of the Thames in 1813,

he was killed, and his dismembered body parts, according to legend, were divided between his conquerors as gruesome souvenirs.

Meanwhile, in 1814, U.S. Gen. Andrew Jackson defeated the British-supported Creeks in the Southwest in the Battle of Horseshoe Bend. The war itself ended in a draw that left American territory intact. Thereafter, with minor exceptions, there was no major Indian resistance east of the Mississippi. After the lusty first quarter century of American nationhood, all roads left open to Native Americans ran downhill.

CONCLUSION

In the roughly half-century between the end of the Great War for the Empire and the War of 1812, the American colonies went from a group of places with economic connections and vague ideas of mutual self-interest to revolutionary confederates to citizens committed to forming a more perfect union. "Join or Die," read a political cartoon created by Benjamin Franklin in 1754 that depicted the colonies as separate parts of a severed snake; by the time of the Revolution, a coiled whole snake had become a popular image of defiant American independence, emblazoned on flags with the words "Don't Tread on Me." Proud and determined, Americans defeated the world's greatest military power to become the United States and fought it again to a draw in the War of 1812 for the right to remain the masters of their own fate. With the Louisiana Purchase, the new country swelled in size. As it grew so did the ambitions of its people, though those ambitions were not always compatible. The land west of the Appalachian Mountains meant one thing for pioneers and another for Native Americans. Cultivation of cotton on a grand scale promised wealth and luxury for the Southern planter class; for those stolen from Africa and their descendants it meant life-long dehumanizing slavery. One man's freedom was not necessarily another man's or woman's freedom. Yet the ideas at the core of the new country's foundation promised freedom for all, and the pursuit of freedom and equality would remain the homing beacon for the American adventure as it unfolded.

Appendices (Documents)

NO TAXATION WITHOUT REPRESENTATION (1765)

Source: *Proceedings of the Congress at New-York*, Boston, 1765: "Saturday, October 19, 1765, AM"

The Congress met according to adjournment, and resumed, etc., as yesterday. And upon mature deliberation agreed to the following declarations of the rights and grievances of the colonists, in America, which were ordered to be inserted.

The members of this Congress, sincerely devoted with the warmest sentiments of affection and duty to His Majesty's person and government, inviolably attached to the present happy establishment of the Protestant succession, and with minds deeply impressed by a sense of the present and impending misfortunes of the British colonies on this continent, having considered as maturely as time will permit the circumstances of the said colonies, esteem it our indispensable duty to make the following declarations of our humble opinion, respecting the most essential rights and liberties of the colonists, and of the grievances under which they labor, by reason of several late acts of Parliament.

- That His Majesty's subjects in these colonies owe the same allegiance to the Crown of Great Britain that is owing from his subjects born within the Realm, and all due subordination to that august body, the Parliament of Great Britain.
- That His Majesty's liege subjects in these colonies are entitled to all the inherent rights and liberties of his natural-born subjects within the Kingdom of Great Britain.
- That it is inseparably essential to the freedom of a people, and the undoubted right of Englishmen, that no taxes be imposed on them but with their own consent, given personally or by their representatives.
- That the people of these colonies are not, and, from their local circumstances, cannot be represented in the House of Commons in Great Britain.
- That the only representatives of the people of these colonies are persons chosen therein by themselves, and that no taxes ever have been or can be constitutionally imposed on them but by their respective legislature.
- That all supplies to the Crown being free gifts of the people, it is unreasonable and inconsistent with the principles and spirit of the British constitution for the people of Great Britain to grant to His Majesty the property of the colonists.

- That trial by jury is the inherent and invaluable right of every British subject in these colonies.
- That the late act of Parliament entitled "An act for granting and applying certain stamp duties, and other duties, in the British colonies and plantations in America, etc.," by imposing taxes on the inhabitants of these colonies, and the said act and several other acts by extending the jurisdiction of the Courts of Admiralty beyond its ancient limits, have a manifest tendency to subvert the rights and liberties of the colonists.
- That the duties imposed by several late acts of Parliament, from the peculiar circumstances of these colonies, will be extremely burdensome and grievous; and from the scarcity of specie, the payment of them absolutely impracticable.
- That as the profits of the trade of these colonies ultimately center in Great Britain to pay for the manufactures which they are obliged to take from thence, they eventually contribute very largely to all supplies granted there to the Crown.
- That the restrictions imposed by several late acts of Parliament on the trade of these colonies will render them unable to purchase the manufactures of Great Britain.
- That the increase, prosperity, and happiness of these colonies depend on the full and free enjoyment of their rights and liberties, and an intercourse with Great Britain mutually affectionate and advantageous.
- That it is the right of the British subjects in these colonies to petition the King or either house of Parliament.

Lastly. That it is the indispensable duty of these colonies, to the best of sovereigns, to the mother country, and to themselves, to endeavor by a loyal and dutiful address to His Majesty and humble applications to both houses of Parliament, to procure the repeal of the act for granting and applying certain stamp duties, of all clauses of any other acts of Parliament whereby the jurisdiction of the Admiralty is extended as aforesaid, and of the other late acts for the restriction of American commerce.

SOAME JENYNS: THE OBJECTIONS TO THE TAXATION OF OUR AMERICAN COLONIES CONSIDERED (1765)

Source: *The Objections to the Taxation of Our American Colonies, by the Legislature of Great Britain, Briefly Consider'd*, 2nd edition, London, 1765.

The right of the legislature of Great Britain to impose taxes on her American colonies, and the expediency of exerting that right in the present conjuncture, are propositions so indisputably clear that I should never have thought it necessary to have undertaken their defense had not many arguments been lately flung out, both in papers and conversation, which with insolence equal to their absurdity deny them both. As these are usually mixed up with several patriotic and favorite words, such as liberty, property, Englishmen, etc., which are apt to make strong impressions on that more numerous part of mankind who have ears but no understanding, it will not, I think, be improper to give them some answers. To this, therefore, I shall singly confine myself, and do it in as few words as possible. ...

The great capital argument, which I find on this subject, and which, like an elephant at the head of a Nabob's army, being once overthrown must put the whole into confusion, is this: that no Englishman is or can be taxed but by his own consent, by which must be meant one of these three propositions — either that no Englishman can be taxed without his own consent as an individual; or that no Englishman can be taxed without the consent of the persons he chooses to represent him; or that no Englishman can be taxed without the consent of the majority of all those who are elected by himself and others of his fellow subjects to represent them. Now, let us impartially consider whether any of these propositions are in fact true. If not, then this wonderful structure which has been erected upon them falls at once to the ground, and like another Babel perishes by a confusion of

words, which the builders themselves are unable to understand.

First, then, that no Englishman is or can be taxed but by his own consent as an individual: this is so far from being true, that it is the very reverse of truth, for no man that I know of is taxed by his own consent; and an Englishman, I believe, is as little likely to be so taxed as any man in the world.

Second, that no Englishman is or can be taxed but by the consent of those persons whom he has chosen to represent him: for the truth of this I shall appeal only to the candid representatives of those unfortunate counties which produce cider and shall willingly acquiesce under their determination.

Lastly, that no Englishman is or can be taxed without the consent of the majority of those who are elected by himself and others of his fellow subjects to represent them: this is certainly as false as the other two, for every Englishman is taxed, and not one in twenty represented: copyholders, leaseholders, and all men possessed of personal property only, choose no representatives. Manchester, Birmingham, and many more of our richest and most flourishing trading towns send no members to Parliament, consequently cannot consent by their representatives because they choose none to represent them. Yet are they not Englishmen? Or are they not taxed?

I am well aware that I shall hear Locke, Sidney, Selden, and many other great names quoted to prove that every Englishman, whether he has a right to vote for a representative or not, is still represented in the British Parliament; in which opinion they all agree. On what principle of common sense this opinion is founded I comprehend not, but on the authority of such respectable names I shall acknowledge its truth; but then I will ask one question, and on that I will rest the whole merits of the cause. Why does not this imaginary representation extend to America as well as over the whole island of Great Britain? If it can travel 300 miles, why not 3,000? If it can jump over rivers and mountains, why cannot it sail over the ocean? If the towns of Manchester and Birmingham, sending no representatives to Parliament, are notwithstanding there represented, why are not the cities of Albany and Boston equally represented in that assembly? Are they not alike British subjects? Are they not Englishmen? Or are they only Englishmen when they solicit for protection, but not Englishmen when taxes are required to enable this country to protect them?

But it is urged that the colonies are by their charters placed under distinct governments, each of which has a legislative power within itself, by which alone it ought to be taxed; that if this privilege is once given up, that liberty which every Englishman has a right to is torn from them, they are all slaves, and all is lost.

The liberty of an Englishman is a phrase of so various a signification, having within these few years been used as a synonymous term for blasphemy, bawdy, treason, libels, strong beer, and cider, that I shall not here presume to define its meaning; but I shall venture to assert what it cannot mean; that is, an exemption from taxes imposed by the authority of the Parliament of Great Britain. Nor is there any charter that ever pretended to grant such a privilege to any colony in America; and had they granted it, it could have had no force, their charters being derived from the Crown, and no charter from the Crown can possibly supersede the right of the whole legislature. Their charters are undoubtedly no more than those of all corporations, which empower them to make bylaws and raise duties for the purposes of their own police, forever subject to the superior authority of Parliament. And in some of their charters, the manner of exercising these powers is specified in these express words, "according to the course of other corporations in Great Britain"; and, therefore, they can have no more pretense to plead an exemption from this parliamentary authority than any other corporation in England.

It has been moreover alleged that, though Parliament may have power to impose taxes on the colonies, they have no right to use it because it would be an unjust tax; and no supreme or legislative power can have a right to enact any law in its nature unjust. To this I shall only make this short reply: that if Parliament can impose no taxes but what are equitable, and the persons taxed are to be the judges of that equity, they will in effect have no power to lay any tax at all. No tax can be imposed exactly equal on all, and if it is not equal, it cannot be just; and if it is not just, no power whatever can impose it; by which short syllogism, all taxation is at an end. But why it should not be used by Englishmen on this side the Atlantic as well as by those on the other I do not comprehend.

THE ASSOCIATION OF THE CONTINENTAL CONGRESS (1774)

Source: *Journals of the American Congress: from 1774 to 1788*, Washington, 1823, Vol. I: "Thursday, October 20, 1774."

We, His Majesty's most loyal subjects, the delegates of the several colonies of New Hampshire, Massachusetts Bay, Rhode Island, Connecticut, New York, New Jersey, Pennsylvania, the three lower counties of Newcastle, Kent, and Sussex on Delaware, Maryland, Virginia, North Carolina, and South Carolina, deputed to represent them in a Continental Congress, held in the city of Philadelphia, on the 5th day of September, 1774, avowing our allegiance to His Majesty, our affection and regard for our fellow subjects in Great Britain and elsewhere, affected with the deepest anxiety and most alarming apprehensions at those grievances and distresses, with which His Majesty's American subjects are oppressed; and having taken under our most serious deliberation the state of the whole continent, find that the present unhappy situation of our affairs is occasioned by a ruinous system of colony administration, adopted by the British Ministry about the year 1763, evidently calculated for enslaving these colonies and with them, the British empire.

In prosecution of which system, various acts of Parliament have been passed for raising a revenue in America; for depriving the American subjects, in many instances, of the constitutional trial by jury; exposing their lives to danger by directing a new and illegal trial beyond the seas for crimes alleged to have been committed in America. And in prosecution of the same system, several late, cruel, and oppressive acts have been passed respecting the town of Boston and the Massachusetts Bay, and also an act for extending the province of Quebec, so as to border on the western frontiers of these colonies, establishing an arbitrary government therein, and discouraging the settlement of British subjects in that wide-extended country; thus, by the influence of civil principles and ancient prejudices to dispose the inhabitants to act with hostility against the free Protestant colonies, whenever a wicked Ministry shall choose to direct them.

To obtain redress of these grievances which threaten destruction to the lives, liberty, and property of His Majesty's subjects in North America, we are of opinion that a nonimportation, nonconsumption, and nonexportation agreement, faithfully adhered to, will prove the most speedy, effectual, and peaceable measure. And, therefore, we do, for ourselves and the inhabitants of the several colonies whom we represent, firmly agree and associate, under the sacred ties of virtue, honor, and love of our country, as follows:

- That from and after the 1st day of December next, we will not import into British America from Great

Britain or Ireland any goods, wares, or merchandise whatsoever, or from any other place, any such goods, wares, or merchandise, as shall have been exported from Great Britain or Ireland. Nor will we, after that day, import any East India tea from any part of the world; nor any molasses, syrups, paneles, coffee, or pimento from the British plantations or from Dominica; nor wines from Madeira or the Western Islands; nor foreign indigo.

- We will neither import nor purchase any slave imported after the 1st day of December next; after which time, we will wholly discontinue the slave trade and will neither be concerned in it ourselves, nor will we hire our vessels, nor sell our commodities or manufactures to those who are concerned in it.

- As a nonconsumption agreement, strictly adhered to, will be an effectual security for the observation of the nonimportation, we, as above, solemnly agree and associate that from this day we will not purchase or use any tea imported on account of the East India Company, or any on which a duty has been or shall be paid. And from and after the 1st day of March next, we will not purchase or use any East India tea whatever; nor will we, nor shall any person for or under us, purchase or use any of those goods, wares, or merchandise we have agreed not to import, which we shall know or have cause to suspect, were imported after the 1st day of December, except such as come under the rules and directions of the 10th Article hereafter mentioned.

- The earnest desire we have not to injure our fellow subjects in Great Britain, Ireland, or the West Indies induces us to suspend a nonexportation [agreement] until the 10th day of September, 1775; at which time, if the said acts and parts of acts of the British Parliament hereinafter mentioned are not repealed, we will not directly or indirectly export any merchandise or commodity whatsoever to Great Britain, Ireland, or the West Indies, except rice to Europe.

- Such as are merchants and use the British and Irish trade will give orders, as soon as possible, to their factors, agents, and correspondents in Great Britain and Ireland not to ship any goods to them, on any pretense whatsoever, as they cannot be received in America; and if any merchant residing in Great Britain or Ireland shall directly or indirectly ship any goods, wares, or merchandise for America in order to break the said nonimportation agreement or in any manner contravene the same, on such unworthy conduct being well attested, it ought to be made public; and, on the same being so done, we will not, from thenceforth, have any commercial connection with such merchant.

- That such as are owners of vessels will give positive orders to their captains or masters not to receive on board their vessels any goods prohibited by the said nonimportation agreement, on pain of immediate dismission from their service.

- We will use our utmost endeavors to improve the breed of sheep and increase their number to the greatest extent; and to that end, we will kill them as seldom as may be, especially those of the most profitable kind; nor will we export any to the West Indies or elsewhere; and those of us who are or may become overstocked with, or can conveniently spare any, sheep will dispose of them to our neighbors, especially to the poorer sort, on moderate terms.

- We will, in our several stations, encourage frugality, economy, and industry, and promote agriculture, arts, and the manufactures of this country, especially that of wool; and will discountenance and discourage every species of extravagance and dissipation, especially all horse racing, and all kinds of gaming, cockfighting, exhibitions of shows, plays, and other expensive diversions and entertainments. And on the death of

any relation or friend, none of us, or any of our families, will go into any further mourning dress than a black crape or ribbon on the arm or hat for gentlemen, and a black ribbon and necklace for ladies, and we will discontinue the giving of gloves and scarves at funerals.

- Such as are vendors of goods or merchandise will not take advantage of the scarcity of goods that may be occasioned by this association, but will sell the same at the rates we have been respectively accustomed to do for twelve months last past. And if any vendor of goods or merchandise shall sell such goods on higher terms, or shall, in any manner or by any device whatsoever, violate or depart from this agreement, no person ought nor will any of us deal with any such person, or his or her factor or agent, at any time thereafter, for any commodity whatever.

- In case any merchant, trader, or other person shall import any goods or merchandise after the 1st day of December and before the 1st day of February next, the same ought forthwith, at the election of the owner, to be either reshipped or delivered up to the committee of the country or town wherein they shall be imported, to be stored at the risk of the importer until the nonimportation agreement shall cease or be sold under the direction of the committee aforesaid. And in the last-mentioned case, the owner or owners of such goods shall be reimbursed out of the sales the first cost and charges, the profit, if any, to be applied toward relieving and employing such poor inhabitants of the town of Boston as are immediate sufferers by the Boston port bill; and a particular account of all goods so returned, stored, or sold to be inserted in the public papers. And if any goods or merchandises shall be imported after the said 1st day of February, the same ought forthwith to be sent back again, without breaking any of the packages thereof.

- That a committee be chosen in every county, city, and town by those who are qualified to vote for representatives in the legislature, whose business it shall be attentively to observe the conduct of all persons touching this association. And when it shall be made to appear, to the satisfaction of a majority of any such committee, that any person within the limits of their appointment has violated this association, that such majority do forthwith cause the truth of the case to be published in the gazette; to the end that all such foes to the rights of British America may be publicly known and universally contemned as the enemies of American liberty; and thenceforth we respectively will break off all dealings with him or her.

- That the Committee of Correspondence, in the respective colonies, do frequently inspect the entries of their customhouses, and inform each other, from time to time, of the true state thereof, and of every other material circumstance that may occur relative to this association.

- That all manufactures of this country be sold at reasonable prices, so that no undue advantage be taken of a future scarcity of goods.

- And we do further agree and resolve that we will have no trade, commerce, dealings, or intercourse whatsoever with any colony or province in North America which shall not accede to, or which shall hereafter violate, this association, but will hold them as unworthy of the rights of freemen and as inimical to the liberties of their country.

And we do solemnly bind ourselves and our constituents, under the ties aforesaid, to adhere to this association until such parts of the several acts of Parliament passed since the close of the last war, as impose or continue duties on tea, wine, molasses, syrups, paneles, coffee, sugar, pimento, indigo, foreign paper, glass, and painters' colors imported into America, and extend the powers of the Admiralty Courts beyond their ancient limits, deprive the American subject of trial by jury, authorize the judge's certificate to indemnify the prosecutor from damages, that he might otherwise be liable to from a trial by his peers, require oppressive security from a claimant of ships or goods seized, before he shall be allowed to defend his property, are repealed.

And until that part of the act ... entitled "An act for the better securing His Majesty's dockyards, magazines, ships, ammunition, and stores," by which any persons charged with committing any of the offenses therein described, in America, may be tried in any shire or county within the Realm, is repealed; and until the four acts, passed the last session of Parliament, viz.: that for stopping the port and blocking up the harbor of Boston; that for altering the charter and government of the Massachusetts Bay; that which is entitled "An act for the better administration of justice, etc.,"; and that "for extending the limits of Quebec, etc.," are repealed. And we recommend it to the provincial conventions, and to the committees in the respective colonies, to establish such further regulations as they may think proper, for carrying into execution this association.

The foregoing association being determined upon by the Congress, was ordered to be subscribed by the several members thereof; and thereupon, we have hereunto set our respective names accordingly.

THE NECESSITY FOR TAKING UP ARMS (1775)

Source: *Journals of the American Congress: from 1774 to 1788*, Washington, 1823, Vol. I: "Thursday, July 6, 1775."

If it was possible for men who exercise their reason to believe that the Divine Author of our existence intended a part of the human race to hold an absolute property in and an unbounded power over others, marked out by His infinite goodness and wisdom, as the objects of a legal domination never rightfully resistible, however severe and oppressive, the inhabitants of these colonies might at least require from the Parliament of Great Britain some evidence that this dreadful authority over them has been granted to that body. But a reverence for our great Creator, principles of humanity, and the dictates of common sense must convince all those who reflect upon the subject that government was instituted to promote the welfare of mankind and ought to be administered for the attainment of that end.

The legislature of Great Britain, however, stimulated by an inordinate passion for a power not only unjustifiable but which they know to be peculiarly reprobated by the very constitution of that kingdom, and desperate of success in any mode of contest where regard should be had to truth, law, or right, have at length, deserting those, attempted to effect their cruel and impolitic purpose of enslaving these colonies by violence, and have thereby rendered it necessary for us to close with their last appeal from reason to arms. Yet, however blinded that assembly may be by their intemperate rage for unlimited domination so to slight justice and the opinion of mankind, we esteem ourselves bound, by obligations of respect to the rest of the world, to make known the justice of our cause.

Our forefathers, inhabitants of the island of Great Britain, left their native land to seek on these shores a residence for civil and religious freedom. At the expense of their blood, at the hazard of their fortunes, without the least charge to the country from which they removed, by unceasing labor and an unconquerable spirit, they effected settlements in the distant and inhospitable wilds of America, then filled with numerous and warlike nations of barbarians. Societies or governments, vested with perfect legislatures, were formed under charters from the Crown, and a harmonious intercourse was established between the colonies and the kingdom from which they derived their origin. The mutual benefits of this union became in a short time so extraordinary as to excite astonishment. It is universally confessed that the amazing increase of the wealth, strength, and navigation of the Realm arose from this source; and the minister, who so wisely and successfully directed the measures of Great Britain in the late war, publicly declared that these colonies enabled her to triumph over her enemies.

Toward the conclusion of that war, it pleased our sovereign to make a change in his counsels. From that fatal moment, the affairs of the British empire began to fall into confusion, and gradually sliding from the summit of glorious prosperity to which they had been advanced by the virtues and abilities of one man, are at length distracted by the convulsions that now shake it to its deepest foundations. The new Ministry finding the brave foes of Britain though frequently defeated yet still contending, took up the unfortunate idea of granting them a hasty peace, and of then subduing her faithful friends.

These devoted colonies were judged to be in such a state as to present victories without bloodshed and all the easy emoluments of statuteable plunder. The uninterrupted tenor of their peaceable and respectful behavior from the beginning of colonization; their dutiful, zealous, and useful services during the war, though so recently and amply acknowledged in the most honorable manner by His Majesty, by the late King, and by Parliament, could not save them from the meditated innovations. Parliament was influenced to adopt the pernicious project, and, assuming a new power over them, have, in the course of eleven years, given such decisive specimens of the spirit and consequences attending this power as to leave no doubt concerning the effects of acquiescence under it. They have undertaken to give and grant our money without our consent, though we have ever exercised an exclusive right to dispose of our own property; statutes have been passed for extending the jurisdiction of Courts of Admiralty and Vice-Admiralty beyond their ancient limits; for depriving us of the accustomed and inestimable privilege of trial by jury, in cases affecting both life and property; for suspending the legislature of one of the colonies; for interdicting all commerce to the capital of another; and for altering fundamentally the form of government established by charter, and secured by acts of its own legislature solemnly confirmed by the Crown; for exempting the "murderers" of colonists from legal trial and, in effect, from punishment; for erecting in a neighboring province, acquired by the joint arms of Great Britain and America, a despotism dangerous to our very existence; and for quartering soldiers upon the colonists in time of profound peace. It has also been resolved in Parliament that colonists charged with committing certain offenses shall be transported to England to be tried.

But why should we enumerate our injuries in detail? By one statute it is declared that Parliament can "of right make laws to bind us in all cases whatsoever." What is to defend us against so enormous, so unlimited a power? Not a single man of those who assume it is chosen by us, or is subject to our control or influence; but, on the contrary, they are all of them exempt from the operation of such laws; and an American revenue, if not diverted from the ostensible purposes for which it is raised, would actually lighten their own burdens in proportion as they increase ours. We saw the misery to which such despotism would reduce us. We for ten years incessantly and ineffectually besieged the throne as supplicants; we reasoned, we remonstrated with Parliament, in the most mild and decent language.

Administration, sensible that we should regard these oppressive measures as freemen ought to do, sent over fleets and armies to enforce them. The indignation of the Americans was roused, it is true; but it was the indignation of a virtuous, loyal, and affectionate people. A congress of delegates from the United Colonies was assembled at Philadelphia, on the 5th day of last September. We resolved again to offer a humble and dutiful petition to the King, and also addressed our fellow subjects of Great Britain. We have pursued every temperate, every respectful measure; we have even proceeded to break off our commercial intercourse with our fellow subjects, as the last peaceable admonition, that our attachment to no nation upon earth should supplant our attachment to liberty. This, we flattered ourselves, was the ultimate step of the controversy; but subsequent events have shown how vain was this hope of finding moderation in our enemies.

Several threatening expressions against the colonies were inserted in His Majesty's speech; our petition, though we were told it was a decent one, and that His Majesty had been pleased to receive it graciously, and to promise laying it before his Parliament, was huddled into both houses among a bundle of American papers and there neglected. The Lords and Commons in their address, in the month of February, said, that "a rebellion at that time actually existed within the province of Massachusetts Bay; and that those concerned in it had been countenanced and encouraged by unlawful combinations and engagements, entered into by His Majesty's subjects in several of the other colonies; and therefore they besought His Majesty that he would take the most effectual measures to enforce due obedience to the laws and authority of the supreme legislature." Soon after, the commercial intercourse of whole colonies with foreign countries, and with each other, was cut off by an act of Parliament; by another, several of them were entirely prohibited from the fisheries in the seas near their coasts, on which they always depended for their sustenance; and large reinforcements of ships and troops were immediately sent over to General Gage.

Fruitless were all the entreaties, arguments, and eloquence of an illustrious band of the most distinguished peers and commoners, who nobly and strenuously asserted the justice of our cause to stay, or even to mitigate, the heedless fury with which these accumulated and unexampled outrages were hurried on. Equally fruitless was the interference of the City of London, of Bristol, and many other respectable towns in our favor. Parliament adopted an insidious maneuver calculated to divide us, to establish a perpetual auction of taxations where colony should bid against colony, all of them uninformed what ransom would redeem their lives; and thus to extort from us, at the point of the bayonet, the unknown sums that should be sufficient to gratify, if possible to gratify, ministerial rapacity, with the miserable indulgence left to us of raising, in our own mode, the prescribed tribute. What terms more rigid and humiliating could have been dictated by remorseless victors to conquered enemies? In our circumstances to accept them would be to deserve them.

Soon after intelligence of these proceedings arrived on this continent, General Gage, who in the course of the last year had taken possession of the town of Boston in the province of Massachusetts Bay, and still occupied it as a garrison, on the 19th day of April, sent out from that place a large detachment of his army, who made an unprovoked assault on the inhabitants of the said province, at the town of Lexington, as appears by the affidavits of a great number of persons, some of whom were officers and soldiers of that detachment, murdered eight of the inhabitants, and wounded many others. From thence the troops proceeded in warlike array to the town of Concord, where they set upon another party of the inhabitants of the same province, killing several and wounding more, until compelled to retreat by the country people suddenly assembled to repel this cruel aggression. Hostilities, thus commenced by the British troops, have been since prosecuted by them without regard to faith or reputation.

The inhabitants of Boston being confined within that town by the general their governor, and having, in order to procure their dismission, entered into a treaty with him, it was stipulated that the said inhabitants having deposited their arms with their own magistrates, should have liberty to depart, taking with them their other effects. They accordingly delivered up their arms; but in open violation of honor, in defiance of the obligation of treaties, which even savage nations esteemed sacred, the governor ordered the arms deposited as aforesaid, that they might be preserved for their owners, to be seized by a body of soldiers; detained the greatest part of the inhabitants in the town, and compelled the few who were permitted to retire to leave their most valuable effects behind. By this perfidy, wives are separated from their husbands, children from their parents, the aged and the sick from their relations and friends who wish to attend and comfort them; and those who have been used to live in plenty and even elegance are reduced to deplorable distress.

The general, further emulating his ministerial masters by a proclamation bearing date on the 12th day of June, after venting the grossest falsehoods and calumnies against the good people of these colonies, proceeds to "declare them all, either by name or description, to be rebels and traitors, to supersede the course of the common law, and instead thereof to publish and order the use and exercise of the law martial." His troops have butchered our countrymen, have wantonly burned Charlestown, besides a considerable number of houses in other places; our ships and vessels are seized; the necessary supplies of provisions are intercepted; and he is exerting his utmost power to spread destruction and devastation around him.

We have received certain intelligence that General Carleton, the governor of Canada, is instigating the people of that province and the Indians to fall upon us; and we have but too much reason to apprehend that schemes have been formed to excite domestic enemies against us. In brief, a part of these colonies now feel, and all of them are sure of feeling, as far as the vengeance of administration can inflict them, the complicated calamities of fire, sword, and famine. We are reduced to the alternative of choosing an unconditional submission to the tyranny of irritated ministers, or resistance by force.

The latter is our choice. We have counted the cost of this contest and find nothing so dreadful as voluntary slavery. Honor, justice, and humanity forbid us tamely to surrender that freedom which we received from our gallant ancestors, and which our innocent posterity have a right to receive from us. We cannot endure the infamy and guilt of resigning succeeding generations to that wretchedness which inevitably awaits them, if we basely entail hereditary bondage upon them.

Our cause is just. Our union is perfect. Our internal resources are great; and, if necessary, foreign assistance is undoubtedly attainable. We gratefully acknowledge, as signal instances of the divine favor toward us, that His providence would not permit us to be called into this severe controversy until we were grown up to our present strength, had been previously exercised in warlike operation, and possessed of the means of defending ourselves. With hearts fortified with these animating reflections, we most solemnly, before God and the world, *declare* that, exerting the utmost energy of those powers which our beneficent Creator has graciously bestowed upon us, the arms we have been compelled by our enemies to assume, we will, in defiance of every hazard, with unabating firmness and perseverance, employ for the preservation of our liberties; being with one mind resolved to die free men rather than live slaves.

Lest this declaration should disquiet the minds of our friends and fellow subjects in any part of the empire, we assure them that we mean not to dissolve that union which has so long and so happily subsisted between us and which we sincerely wish to see restored. Necessity has not yet driven us into that desperate measure, or induced us to excite any other nation to war against them. We have not raised armies with ambitious designs of separating from Great Britain and establishing independent states. We fight not for glory or for conquest. We exhibit to mankind the remarkable spectacle of a people attacked by unprovoked enemies, without any imputation or even suspicion of offense. They boast of their privileges and civilization, and yet proffer no milder conditions than servitude or death.

In our own native land, in defense of the freedom that is our birthright and which we ever enjoyed till the late violation of it, for the protection of our property acquired solely by the honest industry of our forefathers and ourselves, against violence actually offered, we have taken up arms. We shall lay them down when hostilities shall cease on the part of the aggressors and all danger of their being renewed shall be removed, and not before.

With a humble confidence in the mercies of the supreme and impartial Judge and Ruler of the universe, we most devoutly implore His divine goodness to protect us happily through this great conflict, to dispose our adversaries to reconciliation on reasonable terms, and

thereby to relieve the empire from the calamities of civil war.

On a motion made, *Resolved*, that a letter be prepared to the lord mayor, aldermen, and livery of the City of London expressing the thanks of this Congress for their virtuous and spirited opposition to the oppressive and ruinous system of colony administration adopted by the British Ministry.

Ordered, that the committee appointed to draft an address to the people of Great Britain do prepare this.

THOMAS PAINE: PLAIN ARGUMENTS FOR INDEPENDENCE [FROM *COMMON SENSE*] (1776)

Source: *Common Sense*, Boston, 1856.

In the following pages I offer nothing more than simple facts, plain arguments, and common sense; and have no other preliminaries to settle with the reader than that he will divest himself of prejudice and prepossession, and suffer his reason and his feelings to determine for themselves; that he will put *on*, or rather that he will not put *off*, the true character of a man, and generously enlarge his views beyond the present day.

Volumes have been written on the subject of the struggle between England and America. Men of all ranks have embarked in the controversy, from different motives and with various designs; but all have been ineffectual, and the period of debate is closed. Arms, as the last resource, must decide the contest;

the appeal was the choice of the king, and the continent has accepted the challenge.

It has been reported of the late Mr. Pelham (who, though an able minister, was not without his faults) that on his being attacked in the House of Commons, on the score that his measures were only of a temporary kind, replied, "They will last my time." Should a thought so fatal and unmanly possess the colonies in the present contest, the name of ancestors will be remembered by future generations with detestation.

The sun never shone on a cause of greater worth. 'Tis not the affair of a city, a county, a province, or a kingdom but of a continent — of at least one-eighth part of the habitable globe. 'Tis not the concern of a day, a year, or an age; posterity are virtually involved in the contest and will be more or less affected even to the end of time by the proceedings now. Now is the seedtime of continental union, faith, and honor. The least fracture now will be like a name engraved with the point of a pin on the tender rind of a young oak; the wound will enlarge with the tree, and posterity read it in full-grown characters.

By referring the matter from argument to arms, a new area for politics is struck; a new method of thinking has arisen. All plans, proposals, etc., prior to the 19th of April, *i.e.*, to the commencement of hostilities, are like the almanacs of last year; which, though proper then, are superseded and useless now. Whatever was advanced by the advocates on either side of the question then terminated in one and the same point, viz., a union with Great Britain. The only difference between the parties was the method of effecting it, the one proposing force, the other friendship; but it has so far happened that the first has failed, and the second has withdrawn her influence.

As much has been said of the advantages of reconciliation, which, like an agreeable dream, have passed away and left us as we were, it is but right that we should examine the contrary side of the argument, and inquire into some of the many material injuries which these colonies sustain, and always will sustain, by being connected with and dependent on Great Britain. To examine that connection and dependence, on the principles of nature and common sense, to see what we have to trust to if separated, and what we are to expect if dependent.

I have heard it asserted by some that as America has flourished under her former connection with Great Britain, the same connection is necessary toward her future happiness, and will always have the same effect. Nothing can be more fallacious than this kind of argument. We may as well assert that because a child has thrived upon milk ... it is never to have meat, or that the first twenty years of our lives is to become a precedent for the next twenty. But even this is admitting more than is true, for I answer roundly that America would have flourished as much, and probably much more, had no European power had anything to do with her. The articles of commerce, by which she has enriched herself, are the necessaries of life, and will always have a market while eating is the custom of Europe.

But she has protected us, say some. That she has engrossed us is true, and defended the continent at our expense as well as her own is admitted, and she would have defended Turkey from the same motives, viz., for the sake of trade and dominion.

Alas! we have been long led away by ancient prejudices, and made large sacrifices to superstition. We have boasted the protection of Great Britain without considering that her motive was *interest* not *attachment*; and that she did not protect us from *our enemies* on *our account* but from *her enemies* on *her own account,* from those who had no quarrel with us on any *other account*, and who will always be our enemies on the *same account.* Let Britain waive her pretensions to the continent, or the continent throw off the dependence, and we should be at peace with France and Spain, were they at war with Britain. The miseries of Hanover last war ought to warn us against connections.

It has lately been asserted in Parliament that the colonies have no relation to each other but through the parent country, *i.e.,* that Pennsylvania and the Jerseys, and so on for the rest, are sister colonies by the way of England. This is certainly a very roundabout way of proving relationship, but it is the nearest and only true way of proving enemyship, if I may so call it. France and Spain never were, nor perhaps ever will be, our enemies as *Americans* but as our being the *subjects of Great Britain.*

But Britain is the parent country, say some. Then the more shame upon her conduct. Even brutes do not devour their young, nor savages make war upon their families; wherefore, the assertion, if true, turns to her reproach. But it happens not to be true, or only partly so, and the phrase "parent" or "mother country" has been jesuitically adopted by the king and his parasites, with a low papistical design of gaining an unfair bias on the credulous weakness of our minds. Europe, and not England, is the parent country of America. This New World has been the asylum for the persecuted lovers of civil and religious liberty from *every part* of Europe. Hither have they fled, not from the tender embraces of the mother but from the cruelty of the monster; and it is so far true of England that the same tyranny which drove the first emigrants from home pursues their descendants still.

In this extensive quarter of the globe, we forget the narrow limits of 360 miles (the extent of England) and carry our friendship on a larger scale; we claim brotherhood with every European Christian, and triumph in the generosity of the sentiment.

It is pleasant to observe by what regular gradations we surmount local prejudices as we enlarge our acquaintance with the world. A man born in any town in England divided into parishes will naturally associate most with his fellow parishioners (because their interests in many cases will be common) and distinguish him by the name of "neighbor"; if he meet him but a few miles from home, he drops the narrow idea of a street and salutes him by the name of "townsman"; if he travel out of the county and meet him in any other, he forgets the minor divisions of street and town and calls him "countryman," *i.e.*, "countryman." But if in their foreign excursions they should associate in France or any other part of Europe, their local remembrance would be enlarged into that of "Englishmen." And by a just parity of reasoning, all Europeans meeting in America, or any other quarter of the globe, are "countrymen"; for England, Holland, Germany, or Sweden, when compared with the whole, stand in the same places on the larger scale, which the divisions of street, town, and county do on the smaller one — distinctions too limited for continental minds. Not one-third of the inhabitants, even of this province, are of English descent. Wherefore, I reprobate the phrase of "parent" or "mother country" applied to England only as being false, selfish, narrow, and ungenerous.

But, admitting that we were all of English descent, what does it amount to? Nothing. Britain, being now an open enemy, extinguishes every other name and title; and to say that reconciliation is our duty is truly farcical. The first king of England, of the present line (William the Conqueror), was a Frenchman, and half the peers of England are descendants from the same country; wherefore, by the same method of reasoning, England ought to be governed by France.

Much has been said of the united strength of Britain and the colonies — that in conjunction they might bid defiance to the world. But this is mere presumption. The fate of war is uncertain, neither do the expressions mean anything; for this continent would never suffer itself to be drained of inhabitants to support the British arms in either Asia, Africa, or Europe.

Besides, what have we to do with setting the world at defiance? Our plan is commerce, and that, well attended to, will secure us the peace and friendship of all Europe; because it is the interest of all Europe to have America a *free port*. Her trade will always be a protection, and her barrenness of gold and silver secure her from invaders.

I challenge the warmest advocate for reconciliation to show a single advantage that this continent can reap by being connected with Great Britain. I repeat the challenge; not a single advantage is derived. Our corn will fetch its price in any market in Europe, and our imported goods must be paid for, buy them where we will.

But the injuries and disadvantages which we sustain by that connection are without number; and our duty to mankind at large, as well as to ourselves, instructs us to renounce the alliance, because any submission to or dependence on Great Britain tends directly to involve this continent in European wars and quarrels, and sets us at variance with nations who would otherwise seek our friendship, and against whom we have neither anger nor complaint. As Europe is our market for trade, we ought to form no partial connection with any part of it.

It is the true interest of America to steer clear of European contentions which she never can do, while, by her dependence on Britain, she is made the makeweight in the scale of British politics.

Europe is too thickly planted with kingdoms to be long at peace; and whenever a war breaks out between England and any foreign power, the trade of America goes to ruin *because of her connection with Britain.* The next war may not turn out like the last, and should it not, the advocates for reconciliation now will be wishing for separation then, because neutrality in that case would be a safer convoy than a man-of-war. Everything that is right or natural pleads for separation. The blood of the slain, the weeping voice of nature cries, "tis time to part." Even the distance at which the Almighty has placed England and America is a strong and natural proof that the authority of the one over the other was never the design of Heaven. The time, likewise, at which the continent was discovered adds weight to the argument, and the manner in which it was peopled increases the force of it. The Reformation was preceded by the discovery of America, as if the Almighty graciously meant to open a sanctuary to the persecuted in future years, when home should afford neither friendship nor safety.

The authority of Great Britain over this continent is a form of government which sooner or later must have an end; and a serious mind can draw no true pleasure by looking forward, under the painful and positive conviction that what he calls "the present constitution" is merely temporary. As parents, we can have no joy knowing that *this government* is not sufficiently lasting to ensure anything which we may bequeath to posterity; and by a plain method of argument, as we are running the next generation into debt, we ought to do the work of it, otherwise we use them meanly and pitifully. In order to discover the line of our duty rightly, we should take our children in our hand and fix our station a few years further into life; that eminence will present a prospect which a few present fears and prejudices conceal from our sight.

Though I would carefully avoid giving unnecessary offense, yet I am inclined to believe that all those who espouse the doctrine of reconciliation may be included within the following descriptions: Interested men who are not to be trusted; weak men who *cannot* see; prejudiced men who *will not* see; and a certain set of moderate men who think better of the European world than it deserves; and this last class, by an ill-judged deliberation, will be the cause of more calamities to this continent than all the other three.

It is the good fortune of many to live distant from the scene of sorrow; the evil is not sufficiently brought to *their* doors to make *them* feel the precariousness with which all American property is possessed. But let our imaginations transport us a few moments to Boston; that seat of wretchedness will teach us wisdom and instruct us forever to renounce a power in whom we can have no trust. The inhabitants of that unfortunate city, who but a few months ago were in ease and afflu- ence, have now no other alternative than to stay and starve, or turn out to beg. Endangered by the fire of their friends if they continue within the city, and plun- dered by the soldiery if they leave it, in their present situation they are prisoners without the hope of redemption, and in a general attack for their relief, they would be exposed to the fury of both armies.

Men of passive tempers look some- what lightly over the offenses of Britain, and, still hoping for the best, are apt to call out, "Come, come, we shall be friends again for all this." But examine the pas- sions and feelings of mankind, bring the doctrine of reconciliation to the touch- stone of nature, and then tell me whether you can hereafter love, honor, and faith- fully serve the power that has carried fire and sword into your land. If you cannot do all these then are you only deceiving yourselves, and by your delay bringing ruin upon your posterity. Your future connection with Britain, whom you can neither love nor honor, will be forced and unnatural, and being formed only on the plan of present convenience, will in a little time fall into a relapse more wretched than the first. But if you say you can still pass the violations over, then I ask, has your house been burned? Has your property been destroyed before your face? Are your wife and children destitute of a bed to lie on or bread to live on? Have you lost a parent or child by their hands, and yourself the ruined and wretched sur- vivor? If you have not, then are you not a judge of those who have? But if you have,

and can still shake hands with the mur- derers, then are you unworthy the name of husband, father, friend, or lover, and whatever may be your rank or title in life, you have the heart of a coward and the spirit of a sycophant.

This is not inflaming or exaggerating matters but trying them by those feelings and affections which nature justifies, and without which we should be incapable of discharging the social duties of life or enjoying the felicities of it. I mean not to exhibit horror for the purpose of pro- voking revenge but to awaken us from fatal and unmanly slumbers, that we may pursue determinately some fixed object. It is not in the power of Britain or of Europe to conquer America, if she does not conquer herself by *delay* and *timid- ity*. The present winter is worth an age if rightly employed, but if lost or neglected, the whole continent will partake of the misfortune; and there is no punishment which that man will not deserve, be he who or what or where he will, that may be the means of sacrificing a season so pre- cious and useful.

THE DECLARATION OF INDEPENDENCE (1776)

Source: *Journals of the American Congress: from 1774 to 1788*, Washington, 1823, Vol. I: "Thursday, July 4, 1776."

When, in the course of human events, it becomes necessary for one people to dissolve the political bands which have connected them with another, and to assume, among the powers of the earth, the separate and equal station to which the laws of nature and of nature's God entitle them, a decent respect to the opinions of mankind requires that they should declare the causes which impel them to the separation.

We hold these truths to be self-evident, that all men are created equal, that they are endowed by their Creator with certain unalienable rights, that among these are life, liberty, and the pursuit of happiness. That, to secure these rights, governments are instituted among men, deriving their just powers from the consent of the governed. That, whenever any form of government becomes destructive of these ends, it is the right of the people to alter or to abolish it, and to institute new government, laying its foundation on such principles, and organizing its powers in such form, as to them shall seem most likely to effect their safety and happiness.

Prudence, indeed, will dictate that governments long established should not be changed for light and transient causes; and, accordingly, all experience has shown, that mankind are more disposed to suffer, while evils are sufferable, than to right themselves by abolishing the forms to which they are accustomed.

But, when a long train of abuses and usurpations, pursuing invariably the same object, evinces a design to reduce them under absolute despotism, it is their right, it is their duty, to throw off such government, and to provide new guards for their future security. Such has been the patient sufferance of these colonies; and such is now the necessity which constrains them to alter their former systems of government. The history of the present King of Great Britain is a history of repeated injuries and usurpations, all having in direct object the establishment of an absolute tyranny over these states. To prove this, let facts be submitted to a candid world.

He has refused his assent to laws the most wholesome and necessary for the public good.

He has forbidden his governors to pass laws of immediate and pressing importance, unless suspended in their operation till his assent should be obtained; and when so suspended, he has utterly neglected to attend to them.

He has refused to pass other laws for the accommodation of large districts of people, unless those people would relinquish the right of representation in the legislature; a right inestimable to them and formidable to tyrants only.

He has called together legislative bodies at places unusual, uncomfortable, and distant from the depository of their public records, for the sole purpose of fatiguing them into compliance with his measures.

He has dissolved representative houses repeatedly, for opposing, with manly firmness, his invasions on the rights of the people.

He has refused for a long time, after such dissolutions, to cause others to be elected; whereby the legislative powers, incapable of annihilation, have returned to the people at large for their exercise; the state remaining in the meantime exposed to all the dangers of invasion from without, and convulsions within.

He has endeavored to prevent the population of these states; for that purpose obstructing the laws for naturalization of foreigners; refusing to pass others to encourage their migrations hither, and raising the conditions of new appropriations of lands.

He has obstructed the administration of justice, by refusing his assent to laws for establishing judiciary powers.

He has made judges dependent on his will alone, for the tenure of their offices, and the amount and payment of their salaries.

He has erected a multitude of new offices, and sent hither swarms of officers to harass our people, and eat out their substance.

He has kept among us, in times of peace, standing armies, without the consent of our legislatures.

He has affected to render the military independent of and superior to the civil power.

He has combined with others to subject us to a jurisdiction foreign to our constitution, and unacknowledged by our laws; giving his assent to their acts of pretended legislation:

For quartering large bodies of armed troops among us;

For protecting them, by a mock trial, from punishment for any murders which they should commit on the inhabitants of these states;

For cutting off our trade with all parts of the world;

For imposing taxes on us without our consent;

For depriving us, in many cases, of the benefits of trial by jury;

For transporting us beyond seas to be tried for pretended offenses;

For abolishing the free system of English laws in a neighboring province, establishing therein an arbitrary government, and enlarging its boundaries, so as to render it at once an example and fit instrument for introducing the same absolute rule into these colonies;

For taking away our charters, abolishing our most valuable laws, and altering fundamentally the forms of our governments;

For suspending our own legislatures, and declaring themselves invested with power to legislate for us in all cases whatsoever.

He has abdicated government here, by declaring us out of his protection, and waging war against us.

He has plundered our seas, ravaged our coasts, burnt our towns, and destroyed the lives of our people.

He is at this time transporting large armies of foreign mercenaries to complete the works of death, desolation, and tyranny, already begun with circumstances of cruelty and perfidy scarcely paralleled in the most barbarous ages, and totally unworthy the head of a civilized nation.

He has constrained our fellow citizens, taken captive on the high seas, to bear arms against their country, to become the executioners of their friends and brethren, or to fall themselves by their hands.

He has excited domestic insurrections amongst us, and has endeavored to bring on the inhabitants of our frontiers, the merciless Indian savages, whose known rule of warfare is an undistinguished destruction of all ages, sexes, and conditions.

In every stage of these oppressions, we have petitioned for redress, in the most humble terms. Our repeated petitions have been answered only by repeated injury. A prince, whose character is thus marked by every act which may define a tyrant, is unfit to be the ruler of a free people.

Nor have we been wanting in attentions to our British brethren. We have warned them from time to time of attempts by their legislature to extend an unwarrantable jurisdiction over us. We have reminded them of the circumstances of our emigration and settlement here. We have appealed to their native justice and magnanimity, and we have conjured them by the ties of our common kindred, to disavow these usurpations, which would inevitably interrupt our connections and correspondence. They too have been deaf to the voice of justice and of consanguinity. We must, therefore, acquiesce in the necessity, which denounces our separation, and hold them, as we hold the rest of mankind, enemies in war, in peace friends.

We, therefore, the representatives of the United States of America, in General Congress assembled, appealing to the Supreme Judge of the world for the rectitude of our intentions, do, in the name, and by authority of the good people of these colonies, solemnly publish and declare, that these United Colonies are, and of right ought to be free and independent states; that they are absolved from all allegiance to the British Crown, and that all political connection between them and the state of Great Britain is and ought to be totally dissolved; and that, as free and independent states, they have full power to levy war, conclude peace, contract alliances, establish commerce, and to do all other acts and things which independent states may of right do. And for the support of this declaration, with a firm reliance on the protection of Divine Providence, we mutually pledge to each other our lives, our fortunes, and our sacred honor.

GEORGE WASHINGTON: ON THE ORGANIZATION OF THE ARMY (1778)

Source: *The Works of Alexander Hamilton, etc., etc*, John C. Hamilton, ed., New York, 1850–51, Vol. II, "Reorganization of the Army."

The numerous defects in our present military establishment, rendering many reformations and many new arrangements absolutely necessary, and Congress having been pleased to appoint you a committee, in concert with me, to make and recommend such as shall appear eligible, in pursuance of the various objects expressed in the resolution, for that purpose; I have, in the following sheets, briefly delivered my sentiments upon such of them as appeared to me most essential, so far as observation has suggested and leisure permitted. These are submitted to consideration, and I shall be happy, if they are found conducive to remedying the evils and inconveniences we are now subject to, and putting the army upon a more respectable footing. Something must be done; important alterations must be made; necessity requires that our resources should be enlarged and our system improved, for without it, if the dissolution of the army should not be the consequence, at least its operations must be feeble, languid, and ineffectual.

As I consider a proper and satisfactory provision for officers as the basis of every other arrangement and regulation necessary to be made (since without officers no army can exist) and unless some measures be devised to place those officers in a more desirable condition, few of them would be able, if willing, to continue in it. ...

A HALF-PAY AND PENSIONARY ESTABLISHMENT

A small knowledge of human nature will convince us that, with far the greatest part of mankind, interest is the governing principle, and that almost every man is more or less under its influence. Motives of public virtue may, for a time, or in particular instances, actuate men to the observance of a conduct purely disinterested, but

they are not sufficient of themselves to produce a persevering conformity to the refined dictates of social duty. Few men are capable of making a continual sacrifice of all views of private interest or advantage, to the common good. It is in vain to exclaim against the depravity of human nature on this account; the fact is so, the experience of every age and nation has proved it, and we must in a great measure change the constitution of man before we can make it otherwise. No institution not built on the presumptive truth of these maxims can succeed.

We find them exemplified in the American officers as well as in all other men. At the commencement of the dispute, in the first effusions of their zeal, and looking upon the service to be only temporary, they entered into it without paying any regard to pecuniary or selfish considerations. But, finding its duration to be much longer than they at first expected, and that instead of deriving any advantage from the hardships and dangers to which they were exposed, they, on the contrary, were losers by their patriotism, and fell far short even of a competency to supply their wants; they have gradually abated in their ardor, and, with many, an entire disinclination to the service, under its present circumstances, has taken place. To this, in an eminent degree, must be ascribed the frequent resignations daily happening, and the more frequent importunities for permission to resign, and from some officers of the greatest merit. To this also may we ascribe the apathy, inattention, and neglect of duty which pervade all ranks, and which will necessarily continue and increase while an officer, instead of gaining, is impoverished by his commission, and conceives he is conferring, not receiving, a favor in holding it. There can be no tie upon men possessing such sentiments, nor can we adopt any method to oblige those to a punctual discharge of their duty who are indifferent about their continuance in the service, and are often seeking a pretext to disengage themselves from it. Punishment, in this case, will be unavailing; but when an officer's commission is made valuable to him, and he fears to lose it, then may you exact obedience from him.

It is not indeed consistent with reason or justice to expect that one set of men should make a sacrifice of property, domestic ease and happiness, encounter the rigors of the field, the perils and vicissitudes of war to obtain those blessings which every citizen will enjoy in common with them, without some adequate compensation.

It must also be a comfortless reflection to any man that, after he may have contributed to the securing the rights of his country at the risk of his life and the ruin of his fortune, there would be no provision to prevent himself and family from sinking into indigence and wretchedness. I urge these sentiments with the greater freedom because I cannot, and shall not, receive the smallest benefit from the establishment, and have no other inducement for proposing it, than a full conviction of its utility and propriety. ...

OF COMPLETING THE REGIMENTS AND ALTERING THEIR ESTABLISHMENT

The necessity of the first, in the most expeditious manner possible, is too self-evident to need illustrations or proof; and I shall, therefore, only beg leave to offer some reflections on the mode. Voluntary enlistments seem to be totally out of the question; all the allurements of the most exorbitant bounties, and every other inducement that could be thought of, have been tried in vain, and seem to have had little other effect than to increase rapacity and raise the demands of those to whom they were held out. We may fairly infer that the country has been already pretty well drained of that class of men whose tempers, attachments, and circumstances disposed them to enter permanently, or for a length of time, into the army; and that the residue of such men who, from different motives, have kept out of the army, if collected, would not augment our general strength in any proportion to what they require. If experience has demonstrated that little more can be done by voluntary enlistments, some other mode must be concerted, and no other presents itself than that of filling the regiments by drafts from the militia. This is a disagreeable alternative but it is an unavoidable one.

As drafting for the war, or for a term of years, would probably be disgusting and dangerous, perhaps impracticable, I would propose an annual draft of men, without officers, to serve till the 1st day of January in each year. That on or before the 1st day of October preceding, these drafted men should be called upon to reenlist for the succeeding year; and as an incitement to doing it, those being much better and less expensive than raw recruits, a bounty of $25 should be offered. That upon ascertaining at this period the number of men willing to reengage, exact returns should be made to Congress of the deficiency in each regiment and transmitted by them to the respective states, in order that they may have their several quotas immediately furnished and sent on to camp, for the service of the ensuing year, so as to arrive by or before the 1st day of January.

This method, though not so good as that of obtaining men for the war, is perhaps the best our circumstances will allow; and, as we shall always have an established corps of experienced officers, may answer tolerably well. It is the only mode I can think of for completing our battalions in time that promises the least prospect of success; the accomplishment of which is an object of the last importance; and it has this advantage, that the minds of the people being once reconciled to the experiment, it would prove a source of continual supplies hereafter.

Men drafted in this manner should not, in the first instance, receive any bounty from the public; which being solemnly enjoined upon each state, and a stop put to the militia substitution laws, would probably be attended with very happy consequences.

A number of idle mercenary fellows would be thrown out of employment, precluded from their excessive wages as substitutes for a few weeks or months, and constrained to enlist in the Continental Army. In speaking of abolishing the militia substitution laws, it is not meant to hinder a person who might be drafted in the annual allotments from procuring a substitute in his stead, himself in consequence being excused. This indulgence would be admissible, and, considering all things, necessary, as there are many individuals whose dispositions and private affairs would make them irreconcilably averse from giving their personal services for so long a duration, and with whom it would be impolitic to use compulsion. The allowance of substitution upon a smaller scale, in the occasional coming out of the militia for a few weeks, a month or two, is the thing meant to be reprobated. It is highly productive of the double disadvantage of preventing the growth of the army and depreciating our currency....

THE ARTICLES OF CONFEDERATION (1781)

Source: *The Federal and State Constitutions, Colonial Charters, and Other Organic Laws of the United States,* B.P. Poore, ed., Washington, 1877, 2nd edition, Vol. I, pp. 7–12.

Article I. The style of this confederacy shall be "The United States of America."

Article II. Each state retains its sovereignty, freedom, and independence, and every power, jurisdiction, and right which is not by this confederation expressly delegated to the United States in Congress assembled.

Article III. The said states hereby severally enter into a firm league of friendship with each other, for their common defense, the security of their liberties, and their mutual and general welfare, binding themselves to assist each other against all force offered to, or attacks made upon them, or any of them, on account of religion, sovereignty, trade, or any other pretense whatever.

Article IV. The better to secure and perpetuate mutual friendship and intercourse among the people of the different states in this union, the free inhabitants of each of these states, paupers, vagabonds, and fugitives from justice excepted, shall be entitled to all privileges and immunities of free citizens in the several states; and the people of each state shall have free ingress and regress to and from any other state and shall enjoy therein all the privileges of trade and commerce, subject to the same duties, impositions, and restrictions as the inhabitants thereof respectively, provided that such restrictions shall not extend so far as to prevent the removal of property imported into any state, to any other state of which the owner is an inhabitant; provided also that no imposition, duties, or restriction shall be laid by any state on the property of the United States, or either of them.

If any person guilty of or charged with treason, felony, or other high misdemeanor in any state shall flee from justice, and be found in any of the United States, he shall, upon demand of the governor or executive power of the state from which he fled, be delivered up and removed to the state having jurisdiction of his offense.

Full faith and credit shall be given in each of these states to the records, acts, and judicial proceedings of the courts and magistrates of every other state.

Article V. For the more convenient management of the general interests of the United States, delegates shall be annually appointed in such manner as the legislature of each state shall direct, to meet in Congress on the first Monday in November, in every year, with a power reserved to each state to recall its delegates, or any of them, at any time within the year and to send others in their stead for the remainder of the year.

No state shall be represented in Congress by less than two nor by more than seven members; and no person shall be capable of being a delegate for more than three years in any term of six years; nor shall any person, being a delegate, be capable of holding any office under the United States for which he, or another for his benefit, receives any salary, fees, or emolument of any kind.

Each state shall maintain its own delegates in a meeting of the states and while they act as members of the Committee of the States.

In determining questions in the United States in Congress assembled, each state shall have one vote.

Freedom of speech and debate in Congress shall not be impeached or questioned in any court or place out of

Congress, and the members of Congress shall be protected in their persons from arrests and imprisonments during the time of their going to and from, and attendance on, Congress, except for treason, felony, or breach of the peace.

Article VI. No state, without the consent of the United States in Congress assembled, shall send any embassy to, or receive any embassy from, or enter into any conference, agreement, alliance, or treaty with any king, prince, or state; nor shall any person holding any office of profit or trust under the United States, or any of them, accept of any present, emolument, office, or title of any kind whatever from any king, prince, or foreign state; nor shall the United States in Congress assembled, or any of them, grant any title of nobility.

No two or more states shall enter into any treaty, confederation, or alliance whatever between them without the consent of the United States in Congress assembled, specifying accurately the purposes for which the same is to be entered into and how long it shall continue.

No state shall lay any imposts or duties which may interfere with any stipulations in treaties entered into by the United States in Congress assembled with any king, prince, or state, in pursuance of any treaties already proposed by Congress, to the courts of France and Spain.

No vessels of war shall be kept up in time of peace by any state except such number only as shall be deemed necessary by the United States in Congress

assembled for the defense of such state or its trade; nor shall any body of forces be kept up by any state in time of peace except such number only as in the judgment of the United States in Congress assembled shall be deemed requisite to garrison the forts necessary for the defense of such state; but every state shall always keep up a well-regulated and disciplined militia, sufficiently armed and accoutered, and shall provide and constantly have ready for use, in public stores, a due number of field pieces and tents and a proper quantity of arms, ammunition, and camp equipage.

No state shall engage in any war without the consent of the United States in Congress assembled unless such state be actually invaded by enemies, or shall have received certain advice of a resolution being formed by some nation of Indians to invade such state, and the danger is so imminent as not to admit of a delay till the United States in Congress assembled can be consulted; nor shall any state grant commissions to any ships or vessels of war, nor letters of marque or reprisal, except it be after a declaration of war by the United States in Congress assembled, and then only against the kingdom or state and the subjects thereof against which war has been so declared and under such regulations as shall be established by the United States in Congress assembled, unless such state be infested by pirates, in which case vessels of war may be fitted out for that occasion and kept so long as the danger shall continue or until the

United States in Congress assembled shall determine otherwise.

Article VII. When land forces are raised by any state for the common defense, all officers of or under the rank of colonel shall be appointed by the legislature of each state respectively, by whom such forces shall be raised, or in such manner as such state shall direct, and all vacancies shall be filled up by the state which first made the appointment.

Article VIII. All charges of war and all other expenses that shall be incurred for the common defense or general welfare, and allowed by the United States in Congress assembled, shall be defrayed out of a common treasury, which shall be supplied by the several states in proportion to the value of all land within each state, granted to or surveyed for any person, as such land the buildings and improvements thereon shall be estimated according to such mode as the United States in Congress assembled shall from time to time direct and appoint. The taxes for paying that proportion shall be laid and levied by the authority and direction of the legislatures of the several states within the time agreed upon by the United States in Congress assembled.

Article IX. The United States in Congress assembled shall have the sole and exclusive right and power of determining on peace and war, except in the cases mentioned in the sixth article — of sending and receiving ambassadors — entering into treaties and alliances, provided that no treaty of commerce shall be made whereby the legislative power of the respective states shall be restrained from imposing such imposts and duties on foreigners as their own people are subjected to or from prohibiting the exportation or importation of any species of goods or commodities whatsoever — of establishing rules for deciding in all cases what captures on land or water shall be legal, and in what manner prizes taken by land or naval forces in the service of the United States shall be divided or appropriated — of granting letters of marque and reprisal in times of peace — appointing courts for the trial of piracies and felonies committed on the high seas and establishing courts for receiving and determining finally appeals in all cases of captures, provided that no member of Congress shall be appointed a judge of any of the said courts.

The United States in Congress assembled shall also be the last resort on appeal in all disputes and difference now subsisting or that hereafter may arise between two or more states concerning boundary, jurisdiction, or any other cause whatever, which authority shall always be exercised in the manner following: Whenever the legislative or executive authority or lawful agent of any state in controversy with another shall present a petition to Congress stating the matter in question and praying for a hearing, notice thereof shall be given by order of Congress to the legislative or executive authority of the other state in controversy, and a day assigned for the appearance of the parties by their lawful agents, who shall then be directed to appoint, by joint consent, commissioners or judges to constitute a court for hearing and determining the matter in question. But if they cannot agree, Congress shall name three persons out of each of the United States, and from the list of such persons each party shall alternately strike out one, the petitioners beginning, until the number shall be reduced to thirteen. And from that number not less than seven nor more than nine names, as Congress shall direct, shall in the presence of Congress be drawn out by lot, and the persons whose names shall be so drawn, or any five of them, shall be commissioners or judges to hear and finally determine the controversy, so always as a major part of the judges who shall hear the cause shall agree in the determination. ...

If either party shall neglect to attend at the day appointed, without showing reasons, which Congress shall judge sufficient, or being present shall refuse to strike, the Congress shall proceed to nominate three persons out of each state, and the secretary of Congress shall strike in behalf of such party absent or refusing. ... The judgment and sentence of the court to be appointed, in the manner before prescribed, shall be final and conclusive. ... If any of the parties shall refuse to submit to the authority of such court, or to appear or defend their claim or cause, the court shall nevertheless proceed to pronounce sentence or judgment, which shall in like manner be final and decisive, the judgment or sentence and other proceedings being in either case transmitted to Congress and lodged among the acts of Congress for the security of the parties concerned. Provided that every commissioner, before he sits in judgment, shall take an oath to be administered by one of the judges of the supreme or superior court of the state where the cause shall be tried, "well and truly to hear and determine the matter in question, according to the best of his judgment, without favor, affection, or hope of reward": provided, also, that no state shall be deprived of territory for the benefit of the United States.

All controversies concerning the private right of soil claimed under different grants of two or more states, whose jurisdictions as they may respect such lands, and the states which passed such grants are adjusted, the said grants or either of them being at the same time claimed to have originated antecedent to such settlement of jurisdiction shall, on the petition of either party to the Congress of the United States, be finally determined as near as may be in the same manner as is before prescribed for deciding disputes respecting territorial jurisdiction between different states.

The United States in Congress assembled shall also have the sole and exclusive right and power of regulating the alloy and value of coin struck by their own authority or by that of the respective states — fixing the standard of weights and measures throughout the United States — regulating the trade and managing all affairs with the Indians not members of any of the states, provided that the legislative right of any state within its own limits be not infringed or violated — establishing or regulating post offices from one state to another, throughout all the United States, and exacting such postage on the papers passing through the same as may be requisite to defray the expenses of the said office — appointing all officers of the land forces in the service of the United States excepting regimental officers — appointing all the officers of the naval forces, and commissioning all officers whatever in the service of the United States — making rules for the government and regulation of the said land and naval forces, and directing their operations.

The United States in Congress assembled shall have authority to appoint a committee, to sit in the recess of Congress, to be denominated "A Committee of the States," and to consist of one delegate from each state; and to appoint such other committees and civil officers as may be necessary for managing the general affairs of the United States under their direction — to appoint one of their number to preside, provided that no person be allowed to serve in the office of President more than one year in any term of three years; to ascertain the necessary sums of money to be raised for the service of the United States, and to appropriate and apply the same for defraying the public expenses — to borrow money or emit bills on the credit of the United States, transmitting every half-year to the respective states an account of the sums of money so borrowed or emitted — to build and equip a navy — to agree upon the number of land forces, and to make

requisitions from each state for its quota, in proportion to the number of white inhabitants in such state, which requisition shall be binding. ...

Thereupon the legislature of each state shall appoint the regimental officers, raise the men and clothe, arm, and equip them in a soldier-like manner, at the expense of the United States; and the officers and men so clothed, armed, and equipped shall march to the place appointed and within the time agreed on by the United States in Congress assembled. But if the United States in Congress assembled shall, on consideration of circumstances, judge proper that any state should not raise men or should raise a smaller number than its quota and that any other state should raise a greater number of men than the quota thereof, such extra number shall be raised, officered, clothed, armed, and equipped in the same manner as the quota of such state, unless the legislature of such state shall judge that such extra number cannot be safely spared out of the same, in which case they shall raise, officer, clothe, arm, and equip as many of such extra number as they judge can be safely spared. And the officers and men so clothed, armed, and equipped shall march to the place appointed and within the time agreed on by the United States in Congress assembled.

The United States in Congress assembled shall never engage in a war, nor grant letters of marque and reprisal in time of peace, nor enter into any treaties or alliances, nor coin money, nor regulate the value thereof, nor ascertain the sums and expenses necessary for the defense and welfare of the United States, or any of them, nor emit bills, nor borrow money on the credit of the United States, nor appropriate money, nor agree upon the number of vessels of war to be built or purchased or the number of land or sea forces to be raised, nor appoint a commander in chief of the Army or Navy, unless nine states assent to the same; nor shall a question on any other point, except for adjourning from day to day, be determined unless by the votes of a majority of the United States in Congress assembled.

The Congress of the United States shall have power to adjourn to any time within the year, and to any place within the United States, so that no period of adjournment be for a longer duration than the space of six months, and shall publish the journal of their proceedings monthly, except such parts thereof relating to treaties, alliances, or military operations as in their judgment require secrecy; and the yeas and nays of the delegates of each state on any question shall be entered on the journal when it is desired by any delegate; and the delegates of a state, or any of them, at his or their request, shall be furnished with a transcript of the said journal, except such parts as are above excepted, to lay before the legislatures of the several states.

Article X. The Committee of the States, or any nine of them, shall be authorized to execute, in the recess of Congress, such of the powers of Congress as the United States in Congress assembled, by the consent of nine states, shall from time to time think expedient to vest them with; provided that no power be delegated to the said committee, for the exercise of which, by the Articles of Confederation, the voice of nine states in the Congress of the United States assembled is requisite.

Article XI. Canada acceding to this Confederation, and joining in the measures of the United States, shall be admitted into and entitled to all the advantages of this union; but no other colony shall be admitted into the same unless such admission be agreed to by nine states.

Article XII. All bills of credit emitted, moneys borrowed, and debts contracted by or under the authority of Congress, before the assembling of the United States, in pursuance of the present Confederation, shall be deemed and considered as a charge against the United States, for payment and satisfaction whereof the said United States and the public faith are hereby solemnly pledged.

Article XIII. Every state shall abide by the determinations of the United States in Congress assembled on all questions which by this Confederation are submitted to them. And the Articles of this Confederation shall be inviolably observed by every state, and the union shall be perpetual; nor shall any alteration at any time hereafter be made in any of them; unless such alteration be agreed to in a Congress of the United States and be afterward confirmed by the legislatures of every state.

And whereas it has pleased the Great Governor of the world to incline the hearts of the legislatures we respectively represent in Congress to approve of, and to authorize us to ratify the said Articles of Confederation and Perpetual Union. Know ye that we the undersigned delegates, by virtue of the power and authority to us given for that purpose, do by these presents, in the name and in behalf of our respective constituents, fully and entirely ratify and confirm each and every of the said Articles of Confederation and Perpetual Union and all and singular the matters and things therein contained. And we do further solemnly plight and engage the faith of our respective constituents that they shall abide by the determinations of the United States in Congress assembled on all questions which by the said Confederation are submitted to them. And that the articles thereof shall be inviolably observed by the states we respectively represent and that the union shall be perpetual. In witness whereof we have hereunto set our hands in Congress.

THE CONSTITUTION OF VERMONT (1777)

Source: *The Federal and State Constitutions, Colonial Charters, and Other Organic Laws of the United States*, B.P. Poore, ed., Washington, 1877, Vol. II, pp. 1857–1860.

Whereas all government ought to be instituted and supported for the security and protection of the community, as such, and to enable the individuals who compose it to enjoy their natural rights, and other blessings which the Author of existence has bestowed upon man; and whenever those great ends of government are not obtained, the people have a right, by common consent, to change it, and take such measures as to them may appear necessary to promote their safety and happiness;

And whereas the inhabitants of this state have (in consideration of protection only) heretofore acknowledged allegiance to the King of Great Britain, and the said King has not only withdrawn that protection, but commenced, and still continues to carry on, with unabated vengeance, a most cruel and unjust war against them; employing therein not only the troops of Great Britain, but foreign mercenaries, savages and slaves, for the avowed purpose of reducing them to a total and abject submission to the despotic domination of the British Parliament, with many other acts of tyranny (more fully set forth in the declaration of Congress) whereby all allegiance and fealty to the said King and his successors are dissolved and at an end, and all power and authority derived from him ceased in the American colonies.

And whereas the territory which now comprehends the State of Vermont did antecedently, of right, belong to the government of New Hampshire; and the former governor thereof, viz., His Excellency Benning Wentworth, Esq., granted many charters of lands and corporations, within this state, to the present inhabitants and others; *And whereas* the late Lieutenant Governor Colden, of New

York, with others, did, in violation of the tenth command, covet those very lands; and by a false representation made to the court of Great Britain (in the year 1764, that for the convenience of trade and administration of justice, the inhabitants were desirous of being annexed to that government) obtained jurisdiction of those very identical lands *ex parte*; which ever was, and is, disagreeable to the inhabitants; *And whereas* the legislature of New York ever have, and still continue to disown the good people of this state, in their landed property, which will appear in the complaints hereafter inserted, and in the 36th Section of their present constitution, in which is established the grants of land made by that government:

They have refused to make regrants of our lands to the original proprietors and occupants, unless at the exorbitant rate of $2,300 fees for each township; and did enhance the quitrent threefold, and demanded an immediate delivery of the title derived before, from New Hampshire.

The judges of their Supreme Court have made a solemn declaration that the charters, conveyances, etc. of the lands included in the before described premises, were utterly null and void, on which said title was founded: in consequence of which declaration, writs of possession have been by them issued, and the sheriff of the county of Albany sent, at the head of 600 or 700 men, to enforce the execution thereof.

They have passed an act, annexing a penalty thereto, of £ 30 fine and six months imprisonment, on any person who should refuse assisting the sheriff, after being requested, for the purpose of executing writs of possession.

The governors, Dunmore, Tyron, and Colden, have made regrants of several tracts of land included in the premises to certain favorite land jobbers in the government of New York, in direct violation of His Britannic Majesty's express prohibition in the year 1767.

They have issued proclamations, wherein they have offered large sums of money, for the purpose of apprehending those very persons who have dared boldly and publicly to appear in defense of their just rights.

They did pass twelve acts of outlawry, on the 9th day of March, AD 1774, empowering the respective judges of their Supreme Court to award execution of death against those inhabitants in said district that they should judge to be offenders, without trial.

They have, and still continue, an unjust claim to those lands, which greatly retards emigration into, and the settlement of, this state.

They have hired foreign troops, emigrants from Scotland, at two different times, and armed them to drive us out of possession.

They have sent the savages on our frontiers to distress us.

They have proceeded to erect the counties of Cumberland and Gloucester, and establish courts of justice there, after they were discountenanced by the authority of Great Britain.

The free convention of the State of New York, at Harlem, in the year 1776, unanimously voted, "That all quitrents, formerly due to the king of Great Britain, are now due and owing to this convention, or such future government as shall be hereafter established in this state."

In the several stages of the aforesaid oppressions, we have petitioned His Britannic Majesty, in the most humble manner, for redress and have, at very great expense, received several reports in our favor; and, in other instances, wherein we have petitioned the late legislative authority of New York, those petitions have been treated with neglect.

And whereas the local situation of this state, from New York, at the extreme part, is upward of 450 miles from the seat of that government, which renders it extreme difficult to continue under the jurisdiction of said state.

Therefore, it is absolutely necessary, for the welfare and safety of the inhabitants of this state, that it should be, henceforth, a free and independent state; and that a just, permanent, and proper form of government should exist in it, derived from, and founded on, the authority of the people only, agreeable to the direction of the honorable American Congress.

We, the representatives of the freemen of Vermont, in general convention met, for the express purpose of forming such a government — confessing the goodness of the Great Governor of the universe (who alone knows to what degree of earthly happiness mankind may attain, by perfecting the arts of government) in permitting the people of this state, by common consent, and without violence, deliberately to form for themselves such just rules as they shall think best for governing their future society; and being fully convinced that it is our indispensable duty to establish such original principles of government as will best promote the general happiness of the people of this state, and their posterity, and provide for future improvements, without partiality for, or prejudice against, any particular class, sect, or denomination of men whatever — do, by virtue of authority vested in us by our constituents, ordain, declare, and establish the following declaration of rights and frame of government to be the constitution of this Commonwealth, and to remain in force therein, forever unaltered, except in such articles as shall hereafter, on experience, be found to require improvement, and which shall, by the same authority of the people, fairly delegated, as this frame of government directs, be amended or improved, for the more effectual obtaining and securing the great end and design of all government, herein before mentioned.

A DECLARATION OF THE RIGHTS OF THE INHABITANTS OF THE STATE OF VERMONT

- That all men are born equally free and independent, and have certain natural, inherent, and unalienable rights, amongst which are the enjoying and defending life and liberty; acquiring, possessing, and protecting property, and pursuing and obtaining happiness and safety. Therefore, no male person, born in this country or brought from over sea, ought to be holden by law to serve any person as a servant, slave, or apprentice after he arrives to the age of twenty-one years, nor female, in like manner, after she arrives to the age of eighteen years, unless they are bound by their own consent, after they arrive to such age or bound by law, for the payment of debts, damages, fines, costs, or the like.

- That private property ought to be subservient to public uses, when necessity requires it; nevertheless, whenever any particular man's property is taken for the use of the public, the owner ought to receive an equivalent in money.

- That all men have a natural and unalienable right to worship Almighty God according to the dictates of their own consciences and understanding, regulated by the word of God; and that no man ought or of right can be compelled to attend any religious worship, or erect or support any place of worship, or maintain any minister, contrary to the dictates of his conscience; nor can any man who professes the Protestant religion be justly deprived or abridged of any civil right as a citizen on account of his religious sentiment or peculiar mode of religious worship, and that no authority can or ought to be vested in, or assumed by, any power whatsoever, that shall, in any case, interfere with, or in any manner control, the rights of conscience in the free exercise of religious worship; nevertheless, every sect or denomination of people ought to observe the Sabbath, or the Lord's day, and keep up and support some sort of religious worship, which to them shall seem most agreeable to the revealed will of God.

- That the people of this state have the sole, exclusive, and inherent right of governing and regulating the internal police of the same.

- That all power being originally inherent in, and consequently derived from, the people, therefore all officers of government, whether legislative or executive, are their trustees and servants, and at all times accountable to them.

- That government is, or ought to be, instituted for the common benefit, protection, and security of the people, nation or community, and not for the particular emolument or advantage of any single man, family, or set of men who are a part only of that community; and that the community has an indubitable, unalienable, and indefeasible right to reform, alter, or abolish government, in such manner as shall be by that community judged most conducive to the public weal.

- That those who are employed in the legislative and executive business of the state may be restrained from oppression, the people have a right, at such periods as they may think proper, to reduce their public officers to a private station, and supply the vacancies by certain and regular elections.

- That all elections ought to be free; and that all freemen, having a sufficient, evident, common interest with, and attachment to, the community, have a right to elect officers or be elected into office.

- That every member of society has a right to be protected in the enjoyment of life, liberty, and property, and therefore is bound to contribute his proportion toward the expense of that protection, and yield his personal service, when necessary, or an equivalent thereto; but no part of a man's property can be justly taken from him, or applied to public uses, without his own consent or that of his legal representatives; nor can any man who is conscientiously scrupulous of bearing arms be justly compelled thereto, if he will pay such equivalent; nor are the people bound by any law, but such as they have, in like manner, assented to for their common good.

- That in all prosecutions for criminal offenses a man has a right to be heard by himself and his counsel; to demand the cause and nature of his accusation; to be confronted with the witnesses—to call for evidence in his favor, and a speedy public trial by an impartial jury of the country; without the unanimous consent of which jury, he cannot be found guilty; nor can he be compelled to give evidence against himself; nor can any man be justly deprived of his liberty, except by the laws of the land or the judgment of his peers.

- That the people have a right to hold themselves, their houses, papers, and possessions free from search or seizure; and therefore warrants, without oaths or affirmations first made, affording a sufficient foundation for them, and whereby any officer or messenger may be commanded or required to search suspected places, or to seize any person or persons, his, her, or their property, not particularly described, are contrary to that right, and ought not to be granted.

- That no warrant or writ to attach the person or estate of any freeholder within this state shall be issued in civil action without the person or persons who may request such warrant or attachment first make oath, or affirm, before the authority who may be requested to issue the same, that he, or they, are in danger of losing his, her, or their debts.

- That in controversies respecting property, and in suits between man and man, the parties have a right to a trial by jury; which ought to be held sacred.

- That the people have a right to freedom of speech, and of writing and publishing their sentiments; therefore, the freedom of the press ought not be restrained.

- That the people have a right to bear arms for the defense of themselves and the state; and as standing armies, in the time of peace, are dangerous to liberty, they ought not to be kept up; and that the military should be kept under strict subordination to, and governed by, the civil power.

- That frequent recurrence to fundamental principles, and a firm adherence to justice, moderation, temperance, industry, and frugality are absolutely necessary to preserve the blessings of liberty, and keep government free. The people ought, therefore, to pay particular attention to these points, in the choice of officers and representatives, and have a right to exact a due and constant regard to them, from their legislators and magistrates, in the making and executing such laws as are necessary for the good government of the state.

- That all people have a natural and inherent right to emigrate from one state to another that will receive them; or to form a new state in vacant countries, or in such countries as they can purchase, whenever they think that thereby they can promote their own happiness.

- That the people have a right to assemble together; to consult for their common good; to instruct their representatives; and to apply to the legislature for redress of grievances, by address, petition, or remonstrance.

- That no person shall be liable to be transported out of this state for trial for any offense committed within this state.

THE FEDERALIST PAPERS (1787–88)

Source: *The Federalist*, Henry Cabot Lodge, ed., New York, 1888.

ALEXANDER HAMILTON: *THE FEDERALIST* NO. 1

After an unequivocal experience of the inefficiency of the subsisting federal government, you are called upon to deliberate on a new Constitution for the United States of America. The subject speaks its own importance; comprehending in its consequences nothing less than the existence of the Union, the safety and welfare of the parts of which it is composed, the fate of an empire in many respects the most interesting in the world. It has been frequently remarked that it seems to have been reserved to the people of this country, by their conduct and example, to decide the important question, whether societies of men are really capable or not of establishing good government from reflection and choice, or whether they are forever destined to depend for their political constitutions on accident and force. If there be any truth in the remark, the crisis at which we are arrived may with propriety be regarded as the era in which that decision is to be made; and a wrong election of the part we shall act may, in this view, deserve to be considered as the general misfortune of mankind.

This idea will add the inducements of philanthropy to those of patriotism, to heighten the solicitude which all considerate and good men must feel for the event. Happy will it be if our choice should be directed by a judicious estimate of our true interests, unperplexed and unbiased by considerations not connected with the public good. But this is a thing more ardently to be wished than seriously to be expected. The plan offered to our deliberations affects too many particular interests, innovates upon too many local institutions, not to involve in its discussion a variety of objects foreign to its merits, and of views, passions, and prejudices little favorable to the discovery of truth.

Among the most formidable of the obstacles which the new Constitution will have to encounter may readily be distinguished the obvious interest of a certain class of men in every state to resist all changes which may hazard a diminution of the power, emolument, and consequence of the offices they hold under the state establishments; and the perverted ambition of another class of men who will either hope to aggrandize themselves by the confusions of their country or will flatter themselves with fairer prospects of elevation from the subdivision of the empire into several partial confederacies than from its union under one government.

It is not, however, my design to dwell upon observations of this nature. I am well aware that it would be disingenuous to resolve indiscriminately the opposition of any set of men (merely because their situations might subject them to suspicion) into interested or ambitious views. Candor will oblige us to admit that even such men may be actuated by upright intentions; and it cannot be doubted that much of the opposition which has made its appearance, or may hereafter make its appearance, will spring from sources, blameless at least, if not respectable — the honest errors of minds led astray by preconceived jealousies and fears.

So numerous, indeed, and so powerful are the causes which serve to give a false bias to the judgment that we, upon many occasions, see wise and good men on the wrong as well as on the right side of questions of the first magnitude to society. This circumstance, if duly attended to, would furnish a lesson of moderation to those who are ever so much persuaded of their being in the right in any controversy. And a further reason for caution, in this respect, might be drawn from the reflection that we are not always sure that those who advocate the truth are influenced by purer principles than their antagonists. Ambition, avarice, personal animosity, party opposition, and many other motives not more laudable than these, are apt to operate as well upon those who support as those who oppose the right side of a question. Were there not even these inducements to moderation, nothing could be more ill judged than that intolerant spirit which has, at all times, characterized political parties. For in politics, as in religion, it is equally absurd to aim at making proselytes by fire and sword. Heresies in either can rarely be cured by persecution.

And yet, however just these sentiments will be allowed to be, we have already sufficient indications that it will happen in this as in all former cases of great national discussion. A torrent of angry and malignant passions will be let loose. To judge from the conduct of the opposite parties, we shall be led to conclude that they will mutually hope to evince the justness of their opinions, and to increase the number of their converts by the loudness of their declamations and the bitterness of their invectives. An enlightened zeal for the energy and efficiency of government will be stigmatized as the offspring of a temper fond of despotic power and hostile to the principles of liberty.

An overscrupulous jealousy of danger to the rights of the people, which is more commonly the fault of the head than

of the heart, will be represented as mere pretense and artifice, the stale bait for popularity at the expense of public good. It will be forgotten, on the one hand, that jealousy is the usual concomitant of love, and that the noble enthusiasm of liberty is apt to be infected with a spirit of narrow and illiberal distrust. On the other hand, it will be equally forgotten that the vigor of government is essential to the security of liberty; that, in the contemplation of a sound and well-informed judgment, their interest can never be separated; and that a dangerous ambition more often lurks behind the specious mask of zeal for the rights of the people than under the forbidding appearance of zeal for the firmness and efficiency of government. History will teach us that the former has been found a much more certain road to the introduction of despotism than the latter, and that of those men who have over-turned the liberties of republics, the greatest number have begun their career by paying an obsequious court to the people, commencing demagogues and ending tyrants.

In the course of the preceding observations, I have had an eye, my fellow citizens, to putting you upon your guard against all attempts, from whatever quarter, to influence your decision in a matter of the utmost moment to your welfare, by any impressions other than those which may result from the evidence of truth. You will, no doubt, at the same time, have collected from the general scope of them that they proceed from a source not unfriendly to the new Constitution. Yes, my countrymen, I own to you that, after having given it an attentive consideration, I am clearly of opinion it is your interest to adopt it. I am convinced that this is the safest course for your liberty, your dignity, and your happiness. I affect not reserves which I do not feel. I will not amuse you with an appearance of deliberation when I have decided. I frankly acknowledge to you my convictions, and I will freely lay before you the reasons on which they are founded. The consciousness of good intentions disdains ambiguity. I shall not, however, multiply professions on this head. My motives must remain in the depository of my own breast. My arguments will be open to all, and may be judged of by all. They shall at least be offered in a spirit which will not disgrace the cause of truth.

I propose, in a series of papers, to discuss the following interesting particulars: *the utility of the Union to your political prosperity; the insufficiency of the present Confederation to preserve that Union; the necessity of a government at least equally energetic with the one proposed, to the attainment of this object; the conformity of the proposed Constitution to the true principles of republican government; its analogy to your own state constitution; and, lastly, the additional security which its adoption will afford to the preservation of that species of government, to liberty, and to property.*

In the progress of this discussion I shall endeavor to give a satisfactory answer to all the objections, which shall have made their appearance, that may seem to have any claim to your attention.

It may perhaps be thought superfluous to offer arguments to prove the utility of the Union, a point, no doubt, deeply engraved on the hearts of the great body of the people in every state, and one which, it may be imagined, has no adversaries. But the fact is that we already hear it whispered in the private circles of those who oppose the new Constitution that the thirteen states are of too great extent for any general system, and that we must of necessity resort to separate confederacies of distinct portions of the whole. This doctrine will, in all probability, be gradually propagated, till it has votaries enough to countenance an open avowal of it. For nothing can be more evident, to those who are able to take an enlarged view of the subject, than the alternative of an adoption of the new Constitution or a dismemberment of the Union.

JAMES MADISON: *THE FEDERALIST* NO. 14

We have seen the necessity of the Union, as our bulwark against foreign danger, as the conservator of peace among ourselves, as the guardian of our commerce and other common interests, as the only substitute for those military establishments which have subverted the liberties of the Old World, and as the proper antidote for the diseases of faction, which have proved fatal to other popular governments, and of which alarming symptoms have been betrayed by our own. All that remains, within this branch of our inquiries, is to take notice of an objection that may be drawn from the great extent of country which the Union embraces. A few observations on this subject will be the more proper, as it is perceived that the adversaries of the new Constitution are availing themselves of a prevailing prejudice with regard to the practicable sphere of republican administration, in order to supply, by imaginary difficulties, the want of those solid objections which they endeavor in vain to find.

The error which limits republican government to a narrow district has been unfolded and refuted in preceding papers. I remark here only that it seems to owe its rise and prevalence chiefly to the confounding of a republic with a democracy, applying to the former reasonings drawn from the nature of the latter. The true distinction between these forms was also adverted to on a former occasion. It is that, in a democracy, the people meet and exercise the government in person; in a republic, they assemble and administer it by their representatives and agents. A democracy, consequently, will be confined to a small spot. A republic may be extended over a large region.

To this accidental source of the error may be added the artifice of some celebrated authors, whose writings have had a great share in forming the modern standard of political opinions. Being subjects either of an absolute or limited monarchy, they have endeavored to heighten the advantages, or palliate the evils of those forms by placing in comparison the vices and defects of the republican, and by citing as specimens of the latter the turbulent

democracies of ancient Greece and modern Italy. Under the confusion of names, it has been an easy task to transfer to a republic observations applicable to a democracy only; and, among others, the observation that it can never be established but among a small number of people, living within a small compass of territory.

Such a fallacy may have been the less perceived, as most of the popular governments of antiquity were of the democratic species; and even in modern Europe, to which we owe the great principle of representation, no example is seen of a government wholly popular, and founded, at the same time, wholly on that principle. If Europe has the merit of discovering this great mechanical power in government by the simple agency of which the will of the largest political body may be concentrated, and its force directed to any object which the public good requires, America can claim the merit of making the discovery the basis of unmixed and extensive republics. It is only to be lamented that any of her citizens should wish to deprive her of the additional merit of displaying its full efficacy in the establishment of the comprehensive system now under her consideration.

As the natural limit of a democracy is that distance from the central point which will just permit the most remote citizens to assemble as often as their public functions demand, and will include no greater number than can join in those functions; so the natural limit of a republic is that distance from the center which will barely allow the representatives to meet as often as may be necessary for the administration of public affairs. Can it be said that the limits of the United States exceed this distance? It will not be said by those who recollect that the Atlantic coast is the longest side of the Union, that during the term of thirteen years the representatives of the states have been almost continually assembled, and that the members from the most distant states are not chargeable with greater intermissions of attendance than those from the states in the neighborhood of Congress.

That we may form a juster estimate with regard to this interesting subject, let us resort to the actual dimensions of the Union. The limits, as fixed by the treaty of peace, are: on the east the Atlantic, on the south the latitude of 31°, on the west the Mississippi, and on the north an irregular line running in some instances beyond 45°, in others falling as low as 42°. The southern shore of Lake Erie lies below that latitude. Computing the distance between 31° and 45°, it amounts to 973 common miles; computing it from 31° to 42°, to 764½ miles. Taking the mean for the distance, the amount will be 868¾ miles. The mean distance from the Atlantic to the Mississippi does not probably exceed 750 miles.

On a comparison of this extent with that of several countries in Europe, the practicability of rendering our system commensurate to it appears to be demonstrable. It is not a great deal larger than Germany, where a diet representing the whole empire is continually assembled; or than Poland before the late dismemberment, where another national diet was the depositary of the supreme power. Passing by France and Spain, we find that in Great Britain, inferior as it may be in size, the representatives of the northern extremity of the island have as far to travel to the national council as will be required of those of the most remote parts of the Union.

THE BILL OF RIGHTS (1789)

Source: *The Federal and State Constitutions, Colonial Charters, and Other Organic Laws of the United States*, 2nd ed., B.P. Poore, ed., Washington, 1877, Vol. I, pp. 21–22.

ARTICLE I

Congress shall make no law respecting an establishment of religion or prohibiting the free exercise thereof, or abridging the freedom of speech or of the press, or the right of the people peaceably to assemble and to petition the government for a redress of grievances.

ARTICLE II

A well-regulated militia being necessary to the security of a free state, the right of the people to keep and bear arms shall not be infringed.

ARTICLE III

No soldier shall, in time of peace, be quartered in any house without the consent of the owner, nor in time of war but in a manner to be prescribed by law.

ARTICLE IV

The right of the people to be secure in their persons, houses, papers, and effects against unreasonable searches and seizures shall not be violated, and no warrants shall issue, but upon probable cause, supported by oath or affirmation, and particularly describing the place to be searched and the persons or things to be seized.

ARTICLE V

No person shall be held to answer for a capital or otherwise infamous crime unless on a presentment or indictment of a grand jury, except in cases arising in the land or naval forces, or in the militia, when in actual service in time of war or public danger; nor shall any person be subject for the same offense to be twice put in jeopardy of life or limb; nor shall be compelled in any criminal case to be a witness against himself, nor be deprived of life, liberty, or property without due process of law; nor shall private property be taken for public use without just compensation.

ARTICLE VI

In all criminal prosecutions, the accused shall enjoy the right to a speedy and public trial by an impartial jury of the state and district wherein

the crime shall have been committed, which district shall have been previously ascertained by law, and to be informed of the nature and cause of the accusation; to be confronted with the witnesses against him; to have compulsory process for obtaining witnesses in his favor, and to have the assistance of counsel for his defense.

ARTICLE VII

In suits at common law, where the value in controversy shall exceed twenty dollars, the right of trial by jury shall be preserved, and no fact tried by a jury shall be otherwise reexamined in any court of the United States than according to the rules of the common law.

ARTICLE VIII

Excessive bail shall not be required, nor excessive fines imposed, nor cruel and unusual punishments inflicted.

ARTICLE IX

The enumeration in the Constitution of certain rights shall not be construed to deny or disparage others retained by the people.

ARTICLE X

The powers not delegated to the United States by the Constitution, nor prohibited by it to the states, are reserved to the states respectively, or to the people.

PETITION BY FREE AFRICAN AMERICANS FOR EQUALITY UNDER THE LAW (1791)

Source: Manuscript in Slavery File No. 1, Free Persons of Colour, Historical Commission of South Carolina, Columbia.

To the Honorable David Ramsay, Esquire, president, and to the rest of the honorable new members of the Senate of the state of South Carolina,

The memorial of Thomas Cole, bricklayer, P. B. Mathews and Mathew Webb, butchers, on behalf of themselves and others, free men of color, humbly shows:

That in the enumeration of free citizens by the Constitution of the United States for the purpose of representation of the Southern states in Congress your memorialists have been considered under that description as part of the citizens of this state.

Although by the fourteenth and twenty-ninth clauses in an Act of Assembly made in the year 1740 and entitled an Act for the Better Ordering and Governing Negroes and Other Slaves in this Province, commonly called the Negro Act, now in force, your memorialists are deprived of the rights and privileges of citizens by not having it in their power to give testimony on oath in prosecutions on behalf of the state; from which cause many culprits have escaped the punishment due to their atrocious crimes, nor can they give their testimony in recovering debts due to them, or in establishing agreements made by them within the meaning of the Statutes of Frauds and Perjuries in force in this state except in cases where persons of color are concerned, whereby they are subject to great losses and repeated injuries without any means of redress.

That by the said clauses in the said Act, they are debarred of the rights of free citizens by being subject to a trial without the benefit of a jury and subject to prosecution by testimony of slaves without oath by which they are placed on the same footing.

Your memorialists show that they have at all times since the independence of the United States contributed and do now contribute to the support of the government by cheerfully paying their taxes proportionable to their property with others who have been during such period, and now are, in full enjoyment of the rights and immunities of citizens, inhabitants of a free independent state.

That as your memorialists have been and are considered as free citizens of this state, they hope to be treated as such; they are ready and willing to take and subscribe to such oath of allegiance to the states as shall be prescribed by this honorable House, and are also willing to take upon them any duty for the preservation of the peace in the city or any other occasion if called on.

Your memorialists do not presume to hope that they shall be put on an equal footing with the free white citizens of the state in general. They only humbly solicit such indulgence as the wisdom and humanity of this honorable House shall dictate in their favor by repealing the clauses in the Act beforementioned, and substituting such a clause as will effectually redress the grievances which your memorialists humbly submit in this their memorial, but under such restrictions as to your honorable House shall seem proper.

May it therefore please Your Honors to take your memorialists' case into tender consideration, and make such Acts or insert such clauses for the purpose of relieving your memorialists from the unremitted grievance they now labor under as in your wisdom shall seem meet.

ABIGAIL ADAMS: DOUBTS ABOUT INDEPENDENCE (1775)

Source: *Letters of Mrs. Adams, the Wife of John Adams*, Charles Francis Adams, ed., 4th edition, Boston, 1848.

Colonel Warren returned last week to Plymouth, so that I shall not hear anything from you until he goes back again, which will not be till the last of this month. He damped my spirits greatly by telling me that the court had prolonged your stay another month. I was pleasing myself with the thought that you would soon be upon your return. It is in vain to repine. I hope the public will reap what I sacrifice.

I wish I knew what mighty things were fabricating. If a form of government is to be established here, what one will be assumed? Will it be left to our assemblies to choose one? And will not many men have many minds? And shall we not run into dissensions among ourselves?

I am more and more convinced that man is a dangerous creature; and that power, whether vested in many or a few, is ever grasping, and, like the grave, cries "Give, give." The great fish swallow up the small; and he who is most strenuous for the rights of the people when vested with power, is as eager after the prerogatives of government. You tell me of degrees of perfection to which human nature is capable of arriving, and I believe it, but, at the same time, lament that our admiration should arise from the scarcity of the instances.

The building up a great empire, which was only hinted at by my correspondent, may now, I suppose, be realized even by the unbelievers. Yet, will not ten thousand difficulties arise in the formation of it? The reins of government have been so long slackened that I fear the people will not quietly submit to those restraints which are necessary for the peace and security of the community. If we separate from Britain, what code of laws will be established? How shall we be governed so as to retain our liberties? Can any government be free which is not administered by general stated laws? Who shall frame these laws? Who will give them force and energy? It is true your resolutions, as a body, have hitherto had the force of laws; but will they continue to have?

When I consider these things, and the prejudices of people in favor of ancient customs and regulations, I feel anxious for the fate of our monarchy or democracy, or whatever is to take place. I soon get lost in a labyrinth of perplexities; but, whatever occurs, may justice and righteousness be the stability of our times, and order arise out of confusion. Great difficulties may be surmounted by patience and perseverance.

I believe I have tired you with politics. As to news, we have not any at all. I shudder at the approach of winter, when I think I am to remain desolate.

I must bid you good night; 'tis late for me, who am much of an invalid. I was disappointed last week in receiving a packet by the post, and, upon unsealing it, finding only four newspapers. I think you are more cautious than you need be. All letters, I believe, have come safe to hand. I have sixteen from you, and wish I had as many more.

A PLAN OF UNION FOR PROTESTANT CHURCHES (1801)

Source: *A Collection of the Acts, Deliverances, and Testimonies of the Supreme Judicatory of the Presbyterian Church*, Samuel J. Baird, ed., Philadelphia, 1855, pp. 570–571.

Regulations adopted by the General Assembly of the Presbyterian Church in America, and by the General Association of the State of Connecticut (provided said Association agree to them) with a view to prevent alienation and promote union and harmony in those new settlements which are composed of inhabitants from these bodies.

- It is strictly enjoined on all their missionaries to the new settlements to endeavor by all proper means to promote mutual forbearance and a spirit of accommodation between those inhabitants of the new settlements who hold the Presbyterian and those who hold the Congregational form of church government.

- If, in the new settlements, any church of the Congregational order shall settle a minister of the Presbyterian order, that church may, if they choose, still conduct their discipline according to Congregational principles, settling their difficulties among themselves or by a council mutually agreed upon for that purpose. But if any difficulty shall exist between the minister and the church or any member of it, it shall be referred to the presbytery to which the minister shall belong, provided both parties agree to it; if not, to a council consisting of an equal number of Presbyterians and Congregationalists, agreed upon by both parties.

- If a Presbyterian church shall settle a minister of Congregational principles, that church may still conduct their discipline according to Presbyterian principles, excepting that if a difficulty arise between him and his church, or any member of it, the cause shall be tried by the association to which the said minister shall belong, provided both parties agree to it, otherwise by a council, one-half Congregationalists and the other half Presbyterians, mutually agreed upon by the parties.

- If any congregation consist partly of those who hold the Congregational form of discipline and partly of those who hold the Presbyterian form, we recommend to both parties that this be no obstruction to their uniting in one church and settling a minister; and that in this case the church choose a standing committee from the communicants of said church whose business it shall be to call to account every member of the church who shall conduct himself inconsistently with the laws of Christianity, and to give judgment on such conduct. That if the person condemned by their judgment be a Presbyterian, he shall have liberty to appeal to the presbytery; if a Congregationalist, he shall have liberty to appeal to the body of the male communicants of the church. In the former case the determination of the presbytery shall be final, unless the church shall consent to a further appeal to the synod or to the General Assembly; and in the latter case, if the party condemned shall wish for a trial by a mutual council, the cause shall be referred to such a council. And provided the said standing committee of any church shall depute one of themselves to attend the presbytery, he may have the same right to sit and act in the presbytery as a ruling elder of the Presbyterian Church.

GEORGE WASHINGTON: FAREWELL ADDRESS (1796)

Source: *The Writings of George Washington*, Worthington C. Ford, ed., New York, 1889–93, Vol. XIII, pp. 277–325.

Friends and Fellow Citizens:

The period for a new election of a citizen to administer the executive government of the United States being not far distant, and the time actually arrived when your thoughts must be employed in designating the person who is to be clothed with that important trust, it appears to me proper, especially as it may conduce to a more distinct expression of the public voice, that I should now apprise you of the resolution I have formed to decline being considered among the number of those out of whom a choice is to be made.

I beg you, at the same time, to do me the justice to be assured that this resolution has not been taken without a strict regard to all the considerations appertaining to the relation which binds a dutiful citizen to his country; and that, in withdrawing the tender of service which silence in my situation might imply, I am influenced by no diminution of zeal for your future interest, no deficiency of grateful respect for your past kindness, but act under ... a full conviction that the step is compatible with both.

The acceptance of and continuance hitherto in the office to which your suffrages have twice called me have been a uniform sacrifice of inclination to the opinion of duty and to a deference for what appeared to be your desire. I constantly hoped that it would have been much earlier in my power, consistently with motives which I was not at liberty to disregard, to return to that retirement from which I had been reluctantly drawn. The strength of my inclination to do this, previous to the last election, had even led to the preparation of an address to declare it to you; but mature reflection on the then perplexed and critical posture of our affairs with foreign nations, and the unanimous advice of persons entitled to my confidence, impelled me to abandon the idea.

I rejoice that the state of your concerns, external as well as internal, no longer renders the pursuit of inclination incompatible with the sentiment of duty or propriety; and am persuaded, whatever partiality may be retained for my services, that, in the present circumstances of our country, you will not disapprove my determination to retire.

The impressions with which I first undertook the arduous trust were explained on the proper occasion. In the discharge of this trust, I will only say that I have, with good intentions, contributed toward the organization and administration of the government the best exertions of which a very fallible judgment was capable. Not unconscious, in the outset, of the inferiority of my qualifications, experience in my own eyes, perhaps still more in the eyes of others, has strengthened the motives to diffidence of myself; and every day the increasing weight of years admonishes me more and more that the shade of retirement is as necessary to me as it will be welcome. Satisfied that, if any circumstances have given peculiar value to my services, they were temporary, I have the consolation to believe that, while choice and prudence invite me to quit the political scene, patriotism does not forbid it. ...

If benefits have resulted to our country from these services, let it always be remembered to your praise, and as an instructive example in our annals, that, under circumstances in which the passions agitated in every direction were liable to mislead, amidst appearances sometimes dubious, vicissitudes of fortune often discouraging, in situations in which not unfrequently want of success has countenanced the spirit of criticism, the constancy of your support was the essential prop of the efforts and a guarantee of the plans by which they were effected.

Profoundly penetrated with this idea, I shall carry it with me to the grave as a strong incitement to unceasing vows that Heaven may continue to you the choicest tokens of its beneficence; that your Union and brotherly affection may be perpetual; that the free Constitution, which is the work of your hands, may be sacredly maintained; that its administration in every department may be stamped with wisdom and virtue; that, in fine, the happiness of the people of these States, under the auspices of liberty, may be made complete by so careful a preservation and so prudent a use of this blessing as will acquire to them the glory of recommending it to the applause, the affection, and adoption of every nation which is yet a stranger to it.

Here, perhaps, I ought to stop. But a solicitude for your welfare, which cannot end but with my life, and the apprehension of danger natural to that solicitude, urge me, on an occasion like the present, to offer to your solemn contemplation, and to recommend to your frequent review, some sentiments which are the result of much reflection, of no inconsiderable observation, and which appear to me all-important to the permanency of your felicity as a people. These will be offered to you with the more freedom as you can only see in them the disinterested warnings of a parting friend who can possibly have no personal motive to bias his counsels. Nor can I forget, as an encouragement to it, your indulgent reception of my sentiments on a former and not dissimilar occasion.

Interwoven as is the love of liberty with every ligament of your hearts, no recommendation of mine is necessary to fortify or confirm the attachment.

The unity of government which constitutes you one people is also now dear to you. It is justly so, for it is a main pillar in the edifice of your real independence; the support of your tranquillity at home, your peace abroad; of your safety; of your prosperity in every shape; of that very liberty which you so highly prize. But as it is easy to foresee that, from different causes and from different quarters, much pains will be taken, many artifices employed to weaken in your minds the conviction of this truth; as this is the point in your political fortress against which the batteries of internal and external enemies will be most constantly and actively (though often covertly and insidiously) directed, it is of infinite moment that you should properly estimate the immense value of your national Union to your collective and individual happiness; that you should cherish a cordial, habitual, and immovable attachment to it, accustoming yourselves to think and speak of it as of the palladium of your political safety and prosperity, watching for its preservation with jealous anxiety, discountenancing whatever may suggest even a suspicion that it can in any event be abandoned, and indignantly frowning upon the first dawning of every attempt to alienate any portion of our country from the rest or to enfeeble the sacred ties which now link together the various parts.

For this you have every inducement of sympathy and interest. Citizens by birth or choice of a common country, that country has a right to concentrate your affections. The name of *American,* which belongs to you, in your national capacity, must always exalt the just pride of patriotism more than any appellation derived from local discriminations. With slight shades of difference, you have the same religion, manners, habits, and political principles. You have in a common cause fought and triumphed together. The independence and liberty you possess are the work of joint councils and joint efforts, of common dangers, sufferings, and successes.

But these considerations, however powerfully they address themselves to your sensibility, are greatly outweighed by those which apply more immediately to your interest. Here every portion of our country finds the most commanding motives for carefully guarding and preserving the Union of the whole.

The North, in an unrestrained intercourse with the South, protected by the equal laws of a common government, finds in the productions of the latter great additional resources of maritime and commercial enterprise and precious materials of manufacturing industry. The South, in the same intercourse, benefiting by the agency of the North, sees its agriculture grow and its commerce expand. Turning partly into its own channels the seamen of the North, it finds its particular navigation invigorated; and while it contributes, in different ways, to nourish and increase the general mass of the national navigation, it looks forward to the protection of a maritime strength, to which itself is unequally adapted.

The East, in a like intercourse with the West, already finds, and in the progressive improvement of interior communications by land and water will more and more find, a valuable vent for the commodities which it brings from abroad or manufactures at home. The West derives from the East supplies requisite to its growth and comfort, and, what is perhaps of still greater consequence, it must of necessity owe the secure enjoyment of indispensable outlets for its own productions to the weight, influence, and the future maritime strength of the Atlantic side of the Union, directed by an indissoluble community of interest, as *one nation*. Any other tenure by which the West can hold this essential advantage, whether derived from its own separate strength or from an apostate and unnatural connection with any foreign power, must be intrinsically precarious.

While then every part of our country thus feels an immediate and particular interest in Union, all the parts combined in the united mass of means and efforts cannot fail to find greater strength, greater resource, proportionably greater security from external danger, a less frequent interruption of their peace by foreign nations; and — what is of inestimable value! — they must derive from Union an exemption from those broils and wars between themselves which so frequently afflict neighboring countries not tied together by the same government, which their own rivalships alone would be sufficient to produce but which opposite foreign alliances, attachments, and intrigues would stimulate and embitter. Hence, likewise, they will avoid the necessity of those overgrown military establishments which under any form of government are inauspicious to liberty and which are to be regarded as particularly hostile to republican liberty. In this sense it is that your Union ought to be considered as a main prop of your liberty and that the love of the one ought to endear to you the preservation of the other.

These considerations speak a persuasive language to every reflecting and virtuous mind and exhibit the continuance of the *Union* as a primary object of patriotic desire. Is there a doubt whether a common government can embrace so large a sphere? Let experience solve it. To listen to mere speculation in such a case were criminal. We are authorized to hope that a proper organization of the whole, with the auxiliary agency of governments for the respective subdivisions, will afford a happy issue to the experiment. It is well worth a fair and full experiment. With such powerful and obvious motives to Union affecting all parts of our country, while experience shall not have demonstrated its impracticability, there will always be reason to distrust the patriotism of those who in any quarter may endeavor to weaken its bands.

In contemplating the causes which may disturb our Union, it occurs as matter of serious concern that any ground should have been furnished for characterizing parties by geographical discriminations: Northern and Southern; Atlantic and Western; whence designing men may endeavor to excite a belief that there is a real difference of local interests and views. One of the expedients of party to acquire influence, within particular districts, is to misrepresent the opinions and aims of other districts. You cannot shield yourselves too much against the jealousies and heartburnings which spring from these misrepresentations. They tend to render alien to each other those who ought to be bound together by fraternal affection.

The inhabitants of our Western country have lately had a useful lesson on this head. They have seen, in the negotiation by the executive, and in the unanimous ratification by the Senate of the treaty with Spain, and in the universal satisfaction at that event throughout the United States, a decisive proof how unfounded were the suspicions propagated among them of a policy in the general government and in the Atlantic states unfriendly to their interests in regard to the Mississippi. They have been witnesses to the formation of two treaties, that with Great Britain and that with Spain, which secure to them everything they could desire, in respect to our foreign relations, toward confirming their prosperity. Will it not be their wisdom to rely for the preservation of these advantages on the Union by which they were procured? Will they not henceforth be deaf to those advisers, if such there are, who would sever them from their brethren and connect them with aliens?

To the efficacy and permanency of your Union, a government for the whole is indispensable. No alliances, however strict between the parts, can be an adequate substitute. They must inevitably experience the infractions and interruptions which all alliances in all times have experienced. Sensible of this momentous truth, you have improved upon your first essay by the adoption of a Constitution of government better calculated than your former for an intimate Union and for the efficacious management of your common concerns. This government, the offspring of our own choice uninfluenced and unawed, adopted upon full investigation and mature deliberation, completely free in its principles, in the distribution of its powers, uniting security with energy, and containing within itself a provision for its own amendment, has a just claim to your confidence and your support.

Respect for its authority, compliance with its laws, acquiescence in its measures are duties enjoined by the fundamental maxims of true liberty. The basis of our political systems is the right of the people to make and to alter their constitutions of government. But the constitution which at any time exists, till changed by an explicit and authentic act of the whole people, is sacredly obligatory upon all. The very idea of the power and the right of the people to establish government presupposes the duty of every individual to obey the established government.

All obstructions to the execution of the laws, all combinations and associations, under whatever plausible character, with the real design to direct, control, counteract, or awe the regular deliberation and action of the constituted authorities, are destructive of this fundamental principle, and of fatal tendency. They serve to organize faction, to give it an artificial and extraordinary force, to put in the place of the delegated will of the nation the will of a party, often a small but artful and enterprising minority of the community; and, according to the alternate triumphs of different parties, to make the public administration the mirror of the ill-concerted and incongruous projects of faction rather than the organ of consistent and wholesome plans digested by common councils and modified by mutual interests.

However combinations or associations of the above description may now and then answer popular ends, they are likely, in the course of time and things, to become potent engines by which cunning, ambitious, and unprincipled men will be enabled to subvert the power of the people and to usurp for themselves the reins of government, destroying afterward the very engines which have lifted them to unjust dominion.

Toward the preservation of your government and the permanency of your present happy state, it is requisite not only that you steadily discountenance irregular oppositions to its acknowledged authority but also that you resist with care the spirit of innovation upon its principles, however specious the pretexts. One method of assault may be to effect, in the forms of the Constitution, alterations which will impair the energy of the system and thus to undermine what cannot be directly overthrown. In all the changes to which you may be invited, remember that time and habit are at least as necessary to fix the true character of governments as of other human institutions; that experience is the surest standard by which to test the real tendency of the existing constitution of a country; that facility in changes upon the credit of mere hypothesis and opinion exposes to perpetual change, from the endless variety of hypothesis and opinion; and remember, especially, that for the efficient management of your common interests, in a country so extensive as ours, a government of as much vigor as is consistent with the perfect security of liberty is indispensable.

Liberty itself will find in such a government, with powers properly distributed and adjusted, its surest guardian. It is, indeed, little else than a name where the government is too feeble to withstand the enterprises of faction, to confine each member of the society within the limits prescribed by the laws and to maintain all in the secure and tranquil enjoyment of the rights of person and property.

I have already intimated to you the danger of parties in the state, with particular reference to the founding of them on geographical discriminations. Let me now take a more comprehensive view and warn you in the most solemn manner against the baneful effects of the spirit of party generally.

This spirit, unfortunately, is inseparable from our nature, having its root in the strongest passions of the human mind. It exists under different shapes in all governments, more or less stifled, controlled, or repressed; but, in those of the popular form, it is seen in its greatest rankness and is truly their worst enemy.

The alternate domination of one faction over another, sharpened by the spirit of revenge natural to party dissension, which in different ages and countries has perpetrated the most horrid enormities, is itself a frightful despotism. But this leads at length to a more formal and permanent despotism. The disorders and miseries which result gradually incline the minds of men to seek security and repose in the absolute power of an individual; and sooner or later the chief of some prevailing faction, more able or more fortunate than his competitors, turns this disposition to the purposes of his own elevation on the ruins of public liberty.

Without looking forward to an extremity of this kind (which nevertheless ought not to be entirely out of sight), the common and continual mischiefs of the spirit of party are sufficient to make it the interest and duty of a wise people to discourage and restrain it.

It serves always to distract the public councils and enfeeble the public administration. It agitates the community with ill-founded jealousies and false alarms, kindles the animosity of one part against another, foments occasionally riot and insurrection. It opens the door to foreign influence and corruption, which find a facilitated access to the government itself through the channels of party passions. Thus the policy and the will of one country are subjected to the policy and will of another.

There is an opinion that parties in free countries are useful checks upon the administration of the government and serve to keep alive the spirit of liberty. This within certain limits is probably true, and, in governments of a monarchical cast, patriotism may look with indulgence, if not with favor, upon the spirit of party. But in those of the popular character, in governments purely elective, it is a spirit not to be encouraged. From their natural tendency, it is certain there will always be enough of that spirit for every salutary purpose. And there being constant danger of excess, the effort ought to be, by force of public opinion, to mitigate and assuage it. A fire not to be quenched, it demands a uniform vigilance to prevent its bursting into a flame, lest instead of warming it should consume.

It is important, likewise, that the habits of thinking in a free country should inspire caution in those entrusted with its administration to confine themselves within their respective constitutional spheres, avoiding in the exercise of the powers of one department to encroach upon another. The spirit of encroachment tends to consolidate the powers of all the departments in one and thus to create, whatever the form of government, a real despotism. A just estimate of that love of power and proneness to abuse it which predominates in the human heart is sufficient to satisfy us of the truth of this position.

The necessity of reciprocal checks in the exercise of political power, by dividing and distributing it into different depositories, and constituting each the guardian of the public weal against invasions by the others, has been evinced by experiments ancient and modern, some of them in our country and under our own eyes. To preserve them must be as necessary as to institute them. If, in the opinion of the people, the distribution or modification of the constitutional powers be in any particular wrong, let it be corrected by an amendment in the way which the Constitution designates. But let there be no change by usurpation; for, though this, in one instance, may be the instrument of good, it is the customary weapon by which free governments are destroyed. The precedent must always greatly overbalance in permanent evil any partial or transient benefit which the use can at any time yield.

Of all the dispositions and habits which lead to political prosperity, religion and morality are indispensable supports. In vain would that man claim the tribute of patriotism who should labor to subvert these great pillars of human happiness, these firmest props of the duties of men and citizens. The mere politician, equally with the pious man, ought to respect and to cherish them. A volume could not trace all their connections with private and public felicity.

Let it simply be asked—Where is the security for property, for reputation, for life, if the sense of religious obligation desert the oaths, which are the instruments of investigation in courts of justice? And let us with caution indulge the supposition that morality can be maintained without religion. Whatever may be conceded to the influence of refined education on minds of peculiar structure, reason and experience both forbid us to expect that national morality can prevail in exclusion of religious principle.

It is substantially true that virtue or morality is a necessary spring of popular government. The rule indeed extends with more or less force to every species of free government. Who that is a sincere friend to it can look with indifference upon attempts to shake the foundation of the fabric?

Promote, then, as an object of primary importance, institutions for the general diffusion of knowledge. In proportion as the structure of a government gives force to public opinion, it is essential that public opinion should be enlightened.

As a very important source of strength and security, cherish public credit. One method of preserving it is to use it as sparingly as possible, avoiding occasions of expense by cultivating peace, but remembering also that timely disbursements to prepare for danger frequently prevent much greater disbursements to repel it; avoiding likewise the accumulation of debt, not only by shunning occasions of expense but by vigorous exertions in time of peace to discharge the debts which unavoidable wars may have occasioned, not ungenerously throwing upon posterity the burden which we ourselves ought to bear. The execution of these maxims belongs to your representatives, but it is necessary that public opinion should cooperate.

To facilitate to them the performance of their duty, it is essential that you should practically bear in mind that toward the payment of debts there must be revenue; that to have revenue there must be taxes; that no taxes can be devised which are not more or less inconvenient and unpleasant; that the intrinsic embarrassment inseparable from the selection of the proper objects (which is always a choice of difficulties) ought to be a decisive motive for a candid construction of the conduct of the government in making it, and for a spirit of acquiescence in the measures for obtaining revenue which the public exigencies may at any time dictate.

Observe good faith and justice toward all nations. Cultivate peace and harmony with all. Religion and morality enjoin this conduct; and can it be that good policy does not equally enjoin it? It will be worthy of a free, enlightened, and, at no distant period, a great nation to give to mankind the magnanimous and too novel example of a people always guided by an exalted justice and benevolence. Who can doubt that in the course of time and things the fruits of such a plan would richly repay any temporary advantages which might be lost by a steady adherence to it? Can it be that Providence has not connected the permanent felicity of a nation with its virtue? The experiment, at least, is recommended by every sentiment which ennobles human nature. Alas! is it rendered impossible by its vices?

In the execution of such a plan nothing is more essential than that permanent, inveterate antipathies against particular nations and passionate attachments for others should be excluded and that in place of them just and amicable feelings toward all should be cultivated. The nation which indulges toward another an habitual hatred or an habitual fondness is in some degree a slave. It is a slave to its animosity or to its affection, either of which is sufficient to lead it astray from its duty and its interest. Antipathy in one nation against another disposes each more readily to offer insult and injury, to lay hold of slight causes of umbrage, and to be haughty and intractable when accidental or trifling occasions of dispute occur.

Hence, frequent collisions, obstinate, envenomed, and bloody contests. The nation prompted by ill will and resentment sometimes impels to war the government, contrary to the best calculations of policy. The government sometimes participates in the national propensity, and adopts, through passion, what reason would reject; at other times, it makes the animosity of the nation subservient to projects of hostility instigated by pride, ambition, and other sinister and pernicious motives. The peace often, sometimes perhaps the liberty, of nations has been the victim.

So, likewise, a passionate attachment of one nation for another produces a variety of evils. Sympathy for the favorite nation, facilitating the illusion of an imaginary common interest in cases where no real common interest exists, and infusing into one the enmities of the other, betrays the former into a participation in the quarrels and wars of the latter without adequate inducement or justification. It leads also to concessions to the favorite nation of privileges denied to others, which is apt doubly to injure the nation making the concessions, by unnecessarily parting with what ought to have been retained, and by exciting jealousy, ill will, and disposition to retaliate in the parties from whom equal privileges are withheld.

And it gives to ambitious, corrupted, or deluded citizens (who devote themselves to the favorite nation) facility to betray or sacrifice the interests of their own country, without odium, sometimes even with popularity, gilding with the appearances of a virtuous sense of obligation, a commendable deference for public opinion, or a laudable zeal for public good, the base or foolish compliances of ambition, corruption, or infatuation. As avenues to foreign influence in innumerable ways, such attachments are particularly alarming to the truly enlightened and independent patriot. How many opportunities do they afford to tamper with domestic factions, to practise the arts of seduction, to mislead public opinion, to influence or awe the public councils! Such an attachment of a small or weak toward a great and powerful nation dooms the former to be the satellite of the latter.

Against the insidious wiles of foreign influence, I conjure you to believe me, fellow citizens, the jealousy of a free people ought to be *constantly* awake, since history and experience prove that foreign influence is one of the most baneful foes of republican government. But that jealousy, to be useful, must be impartial, else it becomes the instrument of the very influence to be avoided instead of a defense against it. Excessive partiality for one foreign nation and excessive dislike of another cause those whom they actuate to see danger only on one side and serve to veil and even second the arts of influence on the other. Real patriots, who may resist the intrigues of the favorite, are liable to become suspected and odious, while its tools and dupes usurp the applause and confidence of the people to surrender their interests.

The great rule of conduct for us, in regard to foreign nations, is in extending our commercial relations to have with them as little political connection as possible. So far as we have already formed engagements, let them be fulfilled with perfect good faith. Here let us stop.

Europe has a set of primary interests which to us have none, or a very remote relation. Hence she must be engaged in frequent controversies, the causes of which are essentially foreign to our concerns. Hence, therefore, it must be unwise in us to implicate ourselves, by artificial ties, in the ordinary vicissitudes of her politics or the ordinary combinations and collisions of her friendships or enmities.

Our detached and distant situation invites and enables us to pursue a different course. If we remain one people, under an efficient government, the period is not far off when we may defy material injury from external annoyance; when we may take such an attitude as will cause the neutrality we may at any time resolve upon to be scrupulously respected; when belligerent nations, under the impossibility of making acquisitions upon us, will not lightly hazard the giving us provocation; when we may choose peace or war, as our interest guided by our justice shall counsel.

Why forgo the advantages of so peculiar a situation? Why quit our own to stand upon foreign ground? Why, by interweaving our destiny with that of any part of Europe, entangle our peace and prosperity in the toils of European ambition, rivalship, interest, humor, or caprice?

It is our true policy to steer clear of permanent alliances with any portion of the foreign world. So far, I mean, as we are now at liberty to do it, for let me not be understood as capable of patronizing infidelity to existing engagements (I hold the maxim no less applicable to public than to private affairs that honesty is always the best policy). I repeat it, therefore: let those engagements be observed in their genuine sense. But, in my opinion, it is unnecessary and would be unwise to extend them.

Taking care always to keep ourselves, by suitable establishments, on a respectably defensive posture, we may safely trust to temporary alliances for extraordinary emergencies.

Harmony, liberal intercourse with all nations are recommended by policy, humanity, and interest. But even our commercial policy should hold an equal and impartial hand, neither seeking nor granting exclusive favors or preferences; consulting the natural course of things; diffusing and diversifying by gentle means the streams of commerce but forcing nothing; establishing with powers so disposed, in order to give to trade a stable course, to define the rights of our merchants, and to enable the government to support them, conventional rules of intercourse, the best that present circumstances and mutual opinion will permit, but temporary and liable to be from time to time abandoned or varied, as experience and circumstances shall dictate; constantly keeping in view that it is folly in one nation to look for disinterested favors from another; that it must pay with a portion of its independence for whatever it may accept under that character; that, by such acceptance, it may place itself in the condition of having given equivalents for nominal favors and yet of being reproached with ingratitude for not giving more. There can be no greater error than to expect, or calculate, upon real favors from nation to nation. It is an illusion which experience must cure, which a just pride ought to discard.

In offering to you, my countrymen, these counsels of an old and affectionate friend, I dare not hope they will make the strong and lasting impression I could wish; that they will control the usual current of the passions or prevent our nation from running the course which has hitherto marked the destiny of nations. But if I may even flatter myself that they may be productive of some partial benefit, some occasional good; that they may now and then recur to moderate the fury of party-spirit, to warn against the mischiefs of foreign intrigue, to guard against the impostures of pretended patriotism, this hope will be a full recompense for the solicitude for your welfare by which they have been dictated.

In relation to the still subsisting war in Europe, my proclamation of the 22nd of April, 1793, is the index to my plan. Sanctioned by your approving voice and by that of your representatives in both houses of Congress, the spirit of that measure has continually governed me — uninfluenced by any attempts to deter or divert me from it.

After deliberate examination with the aid of the best lights I could obtain, I was well satisfied that our country, under all the circumstances of the case, had a right to take, and was bound in duty and interest to take, a neutral position. Having taken it, I determined, as far as should depend upon me, to maintain it, with moderation, perseverance, and firmness. ...

The inducements of interest for observing that conduct will best be referred to your own reflections and experience. With me, a predominant motive has been to endeavor to gain time to our country to settle and mature its yet recent institutions, and to progress without interruption to that degree of strength and consistency which is necessary to give it, humanly speaking, the command of its own fortune.

Though, in reviewing the incidents of my administration, I am unconscious of intentional error, I am nevertheless too sensible of my defects not to think it probable that I may have committed many errors. Whatever they may be, I fervently beseech the Almighty to avert or mitigate the evils to which they may tend. I shall also carry with me the hope that my country will never cease to view them with indulgence, and that, after forty-five years of my life dedicated to its service, with an upright zeal, the faults of incompetent abilities will be consigned to oblivion as myself must soon be to the mansions of rest.

Relying on its kindness in this as in other things, and actuated by that fervent love toward it which is so natural to a man who views in it the native soil of himself and his progenitors for several generations, I anticipate with pleasing expectations that retreat in which I promise myself to realize, without alloy, the sweet enjoyment of partaking, in the midst of my fellow citizens, the benign influence of good laws under a free government, the ever favorite object of my heart, and the happy reward, as I trust, of our mutual cares, labors, and dangers.

THOMAS JEFFERSON: THE POLITICS OF THE LOUISIANA PURCHASE (1803)

Source: *Memoirs, Correspondence, and Private Papers of Thomas Jefferson*, Thomas Jefferson Randolph, ed., London (and Charlottesville, Va.), 1829, Vol. III, pp. 519–521. *Magazine of American History*, August 1885, p. 199.

I. LETTER TO JOHN BRECKINRIDGE

The enclosed letter ... gives me occasion to write a word to you on the subject of Louisiana, which, being a new one, an interchange of sentiments may produce correct ideas before we are to act on them.

Our information as to the country is very incomplete. We have taken measures to obtain it in full as to the settled part, which I hope to receive in time for Congress. The boundaries, which I deem not admitting question, are the highlands on the western side of the Mississippi enclosing all its waters, the Missouri, of course, and terminating in the line drawn from the northwestern point of the Lake of the Woods to the nearest source of the Mississippi, as lately settled between Great Britain and the United States. We have some claims to extend on the seacoast westwardly to the Rio Norte or Bravo [Rio Grande], and, better, to go eastwardly to the Rio Perdido, between Mobile and Pensacola, the ancient boundary of Louisiana. These claims will be a subject of negotiation with Spain and if, as soon as she is at war, we push them strongly with one hand, holding out a price in the other, we shall certainly obtain the Floridas, and all in good time.

In the meanwhile, without waiting for permission, we shall enter into the exercise of the natural right we have always insisted on with Spain, to wit, that of a nation holding the upper part of streams having a right of innocent passage through them to the ocean. We shall prepare her to see us practise on this, and she will not oppose it by force.

Objections are raising to the eastward against the vast extent of our boundaries, and propositions are made to exchange Louisiana, or a part of it, for the Floridas. But, as I have said, we shall get the Floridas without, and I would not give one inch of the waters of the Mississippi to any nation because I see, in a light very important to our peace, the exclusive right to its navigation, and the admission of no nation into it, but as into the Potomac or Delaware, with our consent and under our police.

These Federalists see in this acquisition the formation of a new confederacy, embracing all the waters of the Mississippi on both sides of it, and a separation of its eastern waters from us. These combinations depend on so many circumstances which we cannot foresee that I place little reliance on them. We have seldom seen neighborhood produce affection among nations. The reverse is almost the universal truth. Besides, if it should become the great interest of those nations to separate from this, if their happiness should depend on it so strongly as to induce them to go through that convulsion, why should the Atlantic states dread it? But, especially, why should we, their present inhabitants, take side in such a question?

When I view the Atlantic states, procuring for those on the eastern waters of the Mississippi friendly instead of hostile neighbors on its western waters, I do not view it as an Englishman would the procuring future blessings for the French nation, with whom he has no relations of blood or affection. The future inhabitants of the Atlantic and Mississippi states will be our sons. We leave them in distinct but bordering establishments. We think we see their happiness in their union, and we wish it. Events may prove it otherwise;

and if they see their interest in separation, why should we take side with our Atlantic rather than our Mississippi descendants? It is the elder and the younger son differing. God bless them both and keep them in union if it be for their good, but separate them if it be better.

The inhabited part of Louisiana, from Point Coupée to the sea, will of course be immediately a territorial government and soon a state. But, above that, the best use we can make of the country for some time will be to give establishments in it to the Indians on the east side of the Mississippi in exchange for their present country, and open land offices in the last, and thus make this acquisition the means of filling up the eastern side instead of drawing off its population. When we shall be full on this side, we may lay off a range of states on the western bank from the head to the mouth, and so, range after range, advancing compactly as we multiply.

This treaty must, of course, be laid before both houses, because both have important functions to exercise respecting it. They, I presume, will see their duty to their country in ratifying and paying for it so as to secure a good which would otherwise probably be never again in their power. But I suppose they must then appeal to the nation for an additional article to the Constitution, approving and confirming an act which the nation had not previously authorized. The Constitution has made no provision for our holding foreign territory, still less for incorporating foreign nations into our Union. The executive, in seizing the fugitive occurrence which so much advances the good of their country, have done an act beyond the Constitution. The legislature in casting behind them metaphysical subtleties, and risking themselves like faithful servants, must ratify and pay for it and throw themselves on their country for doing for them unauthorized what we know they would have done for themselves had they been in a situation to do it.

It is the case of a guardian investing the money of his ward in purchasing an important adjacent territory, and saying to him when of age, I did this for your good; I pretend to no right to bind you; you may disavow me, and I must get out of the scrape as I can; I thought it my duty to risk myself for you. But we shall not be disavowed by the nation, and their act of indemnity will confirm and not weaken the Constitution by more strongly marking out its lines.

II. Letter to Breckinridge

I wrote to you on the 12th inst. on the subject of Louisiana and the constitutional provision that might be necessary for it. A letter received yesterday shows that nothing must be said on that subject which may give a pretext for retracting; but that we should do, *sub silentio*, what shall be found necessary. Be so good, therefore, as to consider that part of my letter as confidential; it strengthens the reasons for desiring the presence of every friend to the treaty on the first day of the session. Perhaps you can impress this necessity on the senators of the Western states by private letter.

Accept my friendly salutations and assurances of great respect and esteem.

III. Proposed Constitutional Amendment

Resolved, by the Senate and House of Representatives of the United States, two-thirds of both houses concurring, that the following amendment to the Constitution of the United States be proposed to the legislatures of the several states, which, when ratified by three-fourths of the said legislatures, shall be valid to all intents and purposes as a part of the said Constitution:

Louisiana, as ceded by France to the United States, is made a part of the United States.

RED JACKET: AGAINST WHITE MISSIONS AMONG THE INDIANS (1805)

Source: *A Library of American Literature*, Edmund C. Stedman and Ellen M. Hutchinson, eds., Vol. IV, New York, 1889, pp. 36–38.

Friend and brother, it was the will of the Great Spirit that we should meet together this day. He orders all things and has given us a fine day for our council. He has taken His garment from before the sun and caused it to shine with brightness upon us. Our eyes are opened, that we see clearly; our ears are unstopped, that we have been able to hear distinctly the words you have spoken. For all these favors we thank the Great Spirit, and Him only.

Brother, this council fire was kindled by you. It was at your request that we came together at this time. We have listened with attention to what you have said. You requested us to speak our minds freely. This gives us great joy, for we now consider that we stand upright before you and can speak what we think. All have heard your voice, and all speak to you now as one man. Our minds are agreed.

Brother, you say you want an answer to your talk before you leave this place. It is right you should have one as you are a great distance from home and we do not wish to detain you. But we will first look back a little and tell you what our fathers have told us and what we have heard from the white people.

Brother, listen to what we say.

There was a time when our forefathers owned this great island. Their seats extended from the rising to the setting sun. The Great Spirit had made it for the use of Indians. He had created the buffalo, the deer, and other animals for food. He had made the bear and the beaver. Their skins served us for clothing. He had scattered them over the country and taught us how to take them. He had caused the earth to produce corn for bread. All this He had done for his red children because He loved them. If we had some disputes about our hunting ground, they were generally settled without the shedding of much blood.

But an evil day came upon us. Your forefathers crossed the great water and landed on this island. Their numbers were small. They found friends and not enemies. They told us they had fled from their own country for fear of wicked men and had come here to enjoy their religion. They asked for a small seat. We took pity on them, granted their request; and they sat down amongst us. We gave them corn and meat; they gave us poison in return.

The white people, brother, had now found our country. Tidings were carried back and more came amongst us. Yet we did not fear them. We took them to be friends. They called us brothers. We believed them and gave them a larger seat. At length their numbers had greatly increased. They wanted more land; they wanted our country. Our eyes were opened and our minds became uneasy. Wars took place. Indians were hired to fight against Indians, and many of our people were destroyed. They also brought strong liquor amongst us. It was strong and powerful and has slain thousands.

Brother, our seats were once large and yours were small. You have now become a great people, and we have scarcely a place left to spread our blankets. You have got our country but are not satisfied; you want to force your religion upon us.

Brother, continue to listen.

You say that you are sent to instruct us how to worship the Great Spirit agreeably to His mind, and, if we do not take hold of the religion which you white people teach, we shall be unhappy hereafter. You say that you are right and we are lost. How do we know this to be true? We understand that your religion is written in a book. If it was intended for us as well as you, why has not the Great Spirit given to us, and not only to us, but why did He not give to our forefathers the knowledge of that book, with the means of understanding it rightly? We only know what you tell us about it. How shall we know when to believe, being so often deceived by the white people?

Brother, you say there is but one way to worship and serve the Great Spirit. If there is but one religion, why do you white people differ so much about it? Why not all agreed, as you can all read the book?

Brother, we do not understand these things. We are told that your religion was given to your forefathers and has been handed down from father to son. We also have a religion which was given to our forefathers and has been handed down to us, their children. We worship in that way. It teaches us to be thankful for all the favors we receive, to love each other, and to be united. We never quarrel about religion.

Brother, the Great Spirit has made us all, but He has made a great difference between His white and red children. He has given us different complexions and different customs. To you He has given the arts. To these He has not opened our eyes. We know these things to be true. Since He has made so great a difference between us in other things, why may

we not conclude that He has given us a different religion according to our understanding? The Great Spirit does right. He knows what is best for His children; we are satisfied.

Brother, we do not wish to destroy your religion or take it from you. We only want to enjoy our own.

Brother, you say you have not come to get our land or our money but to enlighten our minds. I will now tell you that I have been at your meetings and saw you collect money from the meeting. I cannot tell what this money was intended for, but suppose that it was for your minister, and if we should conform to your way of thinking, perhaps you may want some from us.

Brother, we are told that you have been preaching to the white people in this place. These people are our neighbors. We are acquainted with them. We will wait a little while and see what effect your preaching has upon them. If we find it does them good, makes them honest and less disposed to cheat Indians, we will then consider again of what you have said.

Brother, you have now heard our answer to your talk, and this is all we have to say at present. As we are going to part, we will come and take you by the hand and hope the Great Spirit will protect you on your journey and return you safe to your friends.

acquiesce To accept, comply, or submit tacitly or passively.

acrimonious Caustic, biting, or rancorous especially in feeling, language, or manner.

affidavit A sworn statement in writing made especially under oath or on affirmation before an authorized magistrate or officer.

appellation An identifying name or title.

avaricious Greedy of gain; excessively acquisitive, especially in seeking to hoard riches.

conduce To lead or tend to a particular and often desirable result.

constructionist One who construes a legal document (as the United States Constitution) in a specific way.

demagogue A leader who makes use of popular prejudices and false claims and promises in order to gain power.

depredation The act of laying waste, plundering, or ravaging.

diffidence Hesitance in acting or speaking through lack of self-confidence.

divest To deprive or dispossess, especially of property, authority, or title.

embargo A legal prohibition on commerce.

exigency That which is required in a particular situation.

expediency Suitability.

ex post facto After the fact.

fealty The fidelity of a subject to a lord or king; intense fidelity.

felicity The quality or state of being happy.

garrison A military post.

gentry Upper or ruling class.

grievance A cause of distress (as an unsatisfactory working condition) felt to afford reason for complaint or resistance.

habeas corpus A writ for inquiring into the lawfulness of the restraint of a person who is imprisoned or detained in another's custody.

Hessian A German mercenary serving in the British forces during the American Revolution.

imposture The act or practice of deceiving by means of an assumed character or name.

impressment The act of seizing for public use or of impressing into public service.

indubitable Too evident to be doubted.

ingress Entrance.

inordinate Exceeding reasonable limits.

intestate Not disposed of by will.

intransigence The quality or state of refusing to compromise or abandoning an extreme position or attitude.

largesse Generosity.

letters of marque A license granted to a private person to fit out an armed ship to plunder the enemy.

manumission Formal emancipation from slavery.

mercenary Hired for service in the army of a foreign country.

ministerial Being or having the characteristics of an act or duty prescribed by law as part of the duties of an administrative office.

mollify To soothe in temper or disposition.

nascent Coming or having recently come into existence.

obsequious Marked by or exhibiting a fawning attentiveness.

oligarchy A small group exercising control especially for corrupt and selfish purposes.

pecuniary Of or relating to money.

perfidy An act or an instance of disloyalty.

prepossession An attitude, belief, or impression formed beforehand.

presbytery Ruling body in Presbyterian churches consisting of the ministers and representative elders from congregations within a district.

primogeniture An exclusive right of inheritance belonging to the eldest son.

proselyte A new convert (as to a faith or cause).

proviso An article or clause (as in a contract) that introduces a condition.

rapacity The quality or state of being excessively grasping or covetous; rapacious.

rectitude Moral integrity.

regress An act or the privilege of going or coming back.

remonstrate To present and urge reasons in opposition.

repine To feel or express dejection or discontent; complain.

requisition A demand or application made usually with authority.

supplicant One who makes a humble entreaty, especially one who prays to God.

surreptitious Acting or doing something clandestinely.

synod A Presbyterian governing body ranking between the presbytery and the general assembly.

tariff A schedule of duties imposed by a government on imported or, in some countries, exported goods.

unalienable Incapable of being alienated, surrendered, or transferred.

vicissitude The quality or state of being changeable; mutability.

writ of assistance A writ used especially in colonial America authorizing a law officer to search in unspecified locations for unspecified illegal goods.

THE AMERICAN REVOLUTION

Colin G. Calloway, *The Scratch of a Pen: 1763 and the Transformation of North America* (2006), considers how the treaty that ended the Great War for the Empire set the stage for events that followed, including the Revolution. Bernard Bailyn, *The Ideological Origins of the American Revolution*, enlarged ed. (1992); Benjamin L. Carp, *Rebels Rising: Cities and the American Revolution* (2007); Gordon S. Wood, *The Radicalism of the American Revolution* (1992); Joseph J. Ellis, *Founding Brothers: The Revolutionary Generation* (2000); Douglas R. Egerton, *Death or Liberty: African Americans and Revolutionary America* (2009); Gary J. Kornblith, *Slavery and Sectional Strife in the Early American Republic, 1776-1821* (2010); and Richard L. Blanco (ed.), *The American Revolution, 1775–1783: An Encyclopedia*, 2 vol. (1993), are valuable resources. Edward Countryman, *The American Revolution* (1985), considers American social history in the explanation of how *American resistance developed*. T.H. Breen, *American Insurgents, American Patriots: The Revolution of the People* (2010), is a study of the grassroots aspects of the Revolution. P.G.D. Thomas, *British Politics and the Stamp Act Crisis* (1975), is a scholarly account of British objectives and methods, and *The Townshend Duties Crisis* (1987), is the most comprehensive account of this episode. Jerrilyn Greene Marston, *King and Congress* (1987), studies how Congress acquired formal "legitimacy" in the course of rebellion. Pauline Maier, *American Scripture: Making the Declaration of Independence* (1997); and Morton White, *The Philosophy of the American Revolution* (1978), analyze the concepts that took shape in the Declaration of Independence. Jack N. Rakove, *The Beginnings of National Politics* (1979), interprets the complex politics of the Continental Congress.

THE EARLY FEDERAL REPUBLIC

Sean Wilentz, *The Rise of American Democracy: Jefferson to Lincoln* (2005), is an insightful survey. Peter S. Onuf, *The Origins of the Federal Republic* (1983), stresses the jurisdictional problems of relations among states and between states and the Confederation. Gordon S. Wood, *The Creation of the American Republic, 1776-1787* (1969), provides a comprehensive "ideological" interpretation emphasizing the transformation of political thought into action, and *Empire of Liberty: A History of the Early Republic, 1789–1815* (2009), continues the story. David F. Epstein, *The Political Theory of The Federalist* (1984); and the lengthy introduction to Cecelia M. Kenyon, *The Antifederalists* (1966, reprinted 1985), are excellent studies. Jackson Turner Main, *The Antifederalists: Critics of the Constitution, 1781–1788* (1961, reprinted 1974), analyzes the social origins and aspirations of the Anti-Federalists. Joyce Appleby, *Capitalism and a New Social Order* (1984), argues that capitalism was seen as a liberating force by Jeffersonians as well as by Hamiltonians. Other studies of the period include Susan E. Klepp, *Revolutionary Conceptions: Women, Fertility, and Family Limitation in America, 1760–1820* (2009); Anthony F.C. Wallace, *Jefferson and the Indians: The Tragic Fate of the First Americans* (1999); Bernard A. Weisberger, *America Afire: Jefferson, Adams, and the First Contested Election* (2000); James M. Banner, Jr., *To the Hartford Convention: The Federalists and the Origins of Party Politics in Massachusetts, 1789–1815* (1970); John Zvesper, *Political Philosophy and Rhetoric* (1977); and Richard Hofstadter, *The Idea of a Party System* (1969).

INDEX